MILLIONAIRE JANITOR

UNLOCKING THE HIDDEN WEALTH IN EVERYDAY CHOICES

LORN BERGSTRESSER

Millionaire Janitor
Unlocking the Hidden Wealth in Everyday Choices

BERGSTRESSER, LORN, Author
THE MILLIONAIRE JANITOR
LORN BERGSTRESSER

Published by:
ELITE ONLINE PUBLISHING
63 East 11400 South
Suite #230
Sandy, UT 84070
EliteOnlinePublishing.com

ISBN: 978-1-961801-69-1 (Paperback)
ISBN: 978-1-961801-70-7 (eBook)

FIC042060,
FIC045000,
BUS050030

QUANTITY PURCHASES: Schools, companies, professional groups, clubs, and other organizations may qualify for special terms when ordering quantities of this title. For information, email info@lornbergstresser.com

To Laura

DEDICATION & ACKNOWLEDGEMENTS

It's my joy to dedicate this story to my wonderful parents, both of whom were able to live with a positive spirit for over 100 years, raising three children in what their kids didn't realize was poverty. Through their example of hard physical labor, a commitment to honest dealings, and a deep faith, I learned much about how to deal with life and its challenges.

Having read hundreds of books and edited many, writing one was never a serious consideration. This is where Joe Glover, himself an accomplished writer, came into the picture. Through one of life's unexpected meetings, I was introduced to one of the wisest men I've met. It is because of him that this book has come into being. The idea was totally his. Joe's suggestions, based on an intimate knowledge of the book market and his brainchild, "Free Enterprise Warriors", were the sole impetus for this book. Following that encouragement, imagination took over.

Sincere thanks to my exacting proofreaders. The bane of authors (and self-editors) is that their pride (I must call it by its right name), despite every effort to stifle that nasty tendency, is that they too often don't see their own mistakes. I was not immune to this selective blindness.

My hope is that the wisdom demonstrated by the "everyday heroes" in this book will instill guiding life principles in the lives of many young people. Additionally, I hope that succeeding generations and their mentors … parents, teachers, and professors … will absorb and teach the lessons learned by Horatio and Melody. With wisdom and foresight, the young can and will be able to live comfortably while, at the same time, benefiting many who have less.

PRAISE FOR *MILLIONAIRE JANITOR*

"In business and in life, there is a fine line between having the skills and having the mindset to achieve success. The Millionaire Janitor emphasizes the latter. Through meaningful relationships, heartfelt mentorship, and the wisdom of ordinary heroes, Lorn Bergstresser explores the human spirit's power to rise above circumstances. With themes of faith, community, and the rewards of hard work, this story reminds us that success is not always about wealth—sometimes, it's about finding meaning and purpose in the simplest things."

–Stephen Pasiciel, CEO,
Founding Partner of Gryphon Leadership Group
Author of Milestones And How To Avoid Them and Adapt,
Align, Accelerate

"Horatio and Melody are an unexceptional young couple in love but the stars in their eyes don't bedazzle them into making foolish life decisions. Instead, they choose an exceptional path, from educational and career choices, to spending, saving, and giving resolutions to spending, saving and giving. Perfect for young adults who might have received little to no instruction in real-world finance, this quick read flies in the face of today's jaded attitudes toward the American dream. With humor and realism, it offers a rare, timely glimpse of the value of hard work, self-discipline, and character in building wealth over a lifetime."

–Eleanor Bertin, editor and award-winning
author of The Ties That Bind and Burning Bright series.

"Millionaire Janitor" is thoroughly enjoyable-- a positive, necessary message of moral, ethical, spiritual, and financial wisdom invaluable for all, especially young couples starting their marriages. It reminded me of a Bernard Palmer novel about Danny Orlis from my youth, yet written for this generation."

–Mark Middleton
Executive Director (2012-2024), EQUIP Leadership Canada

"Lorn Bergstresser's first foray into novel-writing reveals a unique combination of witty prose and wise life lessons. This love story follows a young couple who demonstrate how lifelong investments in people and finances result in a comfortable retirement and a legacy of positive influence in the lives of many."

–Gordon Giesbrecht, PhD, is a professor emeritus
at the University of Manitoba and is coauthor of the book
Hypothermia, Frostbite and Other Cold Injuries.

"Refreshingly honest and simple financial advice woven into a real-world story to which everyone can relate! Lorn reminds and inspires us that true wealth is attainable by wisely choosing a good financial advisor, setting goals, and then staying the course. A must-read if you are just starting out or a much-needed reminder for those who are years into their wealth-building journeys."

–Jeffrey Klassen MFA,
Senior Financial Advisor, Canada

"While "Millionaire Janitor" is a novel and Melody and Horatio are fictional characters, their story is an inspiration to many of today's young adults who are at the beginning of their marriages and their careers. The critical decisions that they make relative to faith, family, community, work, spending, saving, and financial planning reflect their wisdom and strong character and result in a comfortable retirement and a life of service. Lessons that can be applied to people at every stage of life. My only regret is that the book is a novel. I would love to meet Melody and Horatio in person!"

–Larry J McKinney, Ed.D.,
served as President of Providence University College
and Seminary (MB), Exec. Director of Assoc.
for Biblical Higher Education (FL), and President of
Simpson University (CA). Now a Higher Education Consultant.

TABLE OF CONTENTS

THESE NUMBERS DON'T LIE

Thanks to our nation's amazing Free Enterprise System, the stunning success achieved by Horatio and his wife in pursuing their dream would be unbelievable – if it wasn't for the fact that it continues to happen over and over again!

While our hero is fictional, he is truly representative of millions who have moved from poverty to economic security through their own diligent efforts.

Millionaire Janitor does not present a popular message for those who would have us believe that the American Dream is dead. Nor is this tale for those who confidently assert that there is no point in making the effort to achieve this very realistic aim. Our work has one central, focused, goal – to encourage each individual to understand the rewards awaiting them when they conscientiously pursue their dream.

Based on this clear purpose, on our website we have provided a working spreadsheet which you can download to review the assumptions and calculations used to show Horatio's and Melody's financial progress. You can test these assumptions and even do your own "what-ifs" by going to the link below or scanning the QR code, then downloading the spreadsheet and explanatory document.

Enjoy!

Download the Spreadsheet that explains
Horatio's journey here.
LornBergstresser.com

THE PLAYERS

Horatio Alger Jefferson – the janitor, son of Emily, husband of Melody
Melody Lacoste – wife of Horatio, CPA wannabee
Emily Jefferson – only child of Paul & Stella Jefferson, mother of Horatio
Francois & Annabelle Lacoste – parents of Melody
    Jarvan Grimshaw – father of Horatio
    Brad Parnell – husband of Emily in mid-life
    Angelica Winston – babysitter for Horatio
Aunt Georgina – Emily's widowed aunt with sons Clive, Rattick, and Wolfie

Joseph Radner – principal of Parkview School
    Benjamin Carmichael – retiring head janitor
    Whitt Whittaker – initial assistant to head janitor
    Lola Vang – teacher
    Kevin Martinez – teacher
    Patricia Golding – teacher
    Sophie Quillington - teacher
    Rory Janvier – student
    Emmanuel Irvine – student
    Colleen Koolidge – student
    Cherry Treadly – student

Interviewees for Assistant Janitor
    Harriman Bumblethwaite
    Molly Dunbar
    Serena Blake
    Bill Withers
    Jeff Monahan

Wilfred Williams – pastor
    Karena "Kari" Williams – wife of Wilfred
    Darrell Williams – Wilfred's brother

Lamar Brooks – bank loans officer

Nadia Gentille – medical doctor

Windy City Financial Services
    Anthony Scrivens – president and CEO
        Arnold Kinkaid – childhood friend of Anthony
    Receptionist – Willow Bertsch
    Betsy Watkins – Melody's supervisor
    CPAs – Cedric Ravenshadow
        – Higgins, Bartelli, Washington, Davis

Verna Newman – owner of Urban Elegance

Isabella Chavez – chief steward at Great Lakes Financial Stewards

Darius Thompson – manager of Bluebird Apartments
Odell Wigglesworth – owner of Bluebird Apartments

Fire Chief – Diego Valdez
    Police – Sgt. Brock Bigelow
        – Const. Susan Workman

CHAPTER 1

CRADLE OF DREAMS AND DESPAIR

In the heart of South Chicago, where the streets normally echoed with the rhythm of life and the pulse of the city, a miraculously normal event unfolded on a bitterly cold February night. It was a night when the frost seemed to cling to the air, weaving its icy tendrils through the alleys and around the corners of the modest buildings that lined the streets. To call the rows of identical duplexes "modest" is, to be accurate, an exaggeration of their attractiveness. Realistically, the entire neighborhood may well have been described, at best, as middle-lower class. Many, in more affluent districts, would have referred to the environs as "the slums". Yet, even there, life went on. Honest people were eking out an honest living. The dishonest were doing what dishonest people do. Not that different from their richer fellow Chicagoans.

In the midst of this wintry and somewhat depressing tableau, aided by the local midwife, and following the normal nine months during which the child prepared for birth, a new person became visible to the world. Horatio Alger Jefferson let out a cry as he took his first breath in a world blanketed in snow, his arrival marking a moment of both joy and uncertainty. His mother, Emily Jefferson, a 17-year-old girl of petite stature but immeasurable strength of character, welcomed her son into the world with a mixture of mother's love, awe, and determination. Emily named her son as she did, remembering her enjoyment of the works of the famous novelist in her 10th, and last, year in school. Alger's stories of rags-to-riches had always fascinated Emily.

Emily herself had experienced traumatic early teen years, her parents (Paul and Stella) having both died within a year of each other. Paul and Stella had been pillars of integrity in their community. That honorable quality showed itself in their raising of little Emily. "Sure, Emily, we are poor, and we'll never be able to live in Edison Park or dine at Mastro's Steakhouse, but we are blessed to have what we have" … and then her father would say, "Emily, don't ever succumb to the dogma of victim theology. Government is not God, so don't depend on it." And another of her father's favorite sayings was, "Keep on the right track, and it'll all turn out for the best." Paul had been a plumber and, while on the job, had been in the wrong place at the wrong time. Suffice it to say, he was caught in the crossfire. Some months before Paul's sudden death, Stella had been diagnosed with cancer. She died just 360 days after her husband's passing. Emily was left on her own, without siblings, but with a determined will to survive. At times, though, she wondered about her dad's "It'll all turn out for the best." Mother and father had invested both love and practical knowledge into the life of their little girl.

The small home her parents had purchased 10 years earlier became Emily's. She had been only 14 at the time; two kindly ladies from social services had arrived at her door and interviewed her shortly after her mother's funeral. Their intent had been to place her in a foster home but, when speaking with her, they quickly realized that they were dealing with a young lady who, in terms of maturity and ability, was far beyond her years. They then showed up from time to time – the checkups initially were spaced in three-week intervals. After that, however, they checked in with her quarterly, once again when she was 15 ½, and then not at all. Her parents had left her enough in their wills to enable her to exist for about 16 months.

Although her widowed Aunt Georgina, who lived 'somewhere in the country', had offered to take her in, Emily declined, as her aunt had only sons, two of whom were Clive & Rattick - their reputations were not impeccable. In fact, these older two appeared to have acquired ill-gotten gains that could not possibly have been earned on the back street "bicycle shop" where they claimed to work. The youngest son (Wolfie), Emily's age, always made the hair on the nape of her neck stand up when she was alone with him. Goodhearted Aunt Georgina was able, however, to provide Emily a small monthly allowance "until you can get on your feet". This was a big help for Emily, as her "inheritance" would run out quickly.

It had been about two years after Stella's death when 23-year-old Jarvan Grimshaw ("white trash" as some of his darker-skinned neighbors called him) had shown up, showing sympathy and what she really believed was love. She knew nothing of his background – except for the lies he told her. Not only was he handsome, but he also said all the right things. Emily was alone in the world and, in a moment of weakness, fell for his charm. In light of the tragic death of her parents and the resulting trauma, he promised to stand by Emily's side through thick and thin but, upon discovering the news of her pregnancy, had fled Chicago for parts unknown. He was never heard from again … at least not directly. Apparently, Aunt Georgina did know something of Jarvan's whereabouts (he'd gotten along well with Clive and Rattick); some years later, shortly before she passed away, she told Emily that Jarvan had moved to Sebring, Florida; he had worked for a while at the Sebring Raceway where, unfortunately, he had arrived at the site 'under the influence' and had stumbled, falling into the path of a vehicle speeding into a pit stop, in the middle of the 11th hour of the "12 Hours of Sebring" event. Apparently, he had left two wives to mourn his passing. There were rumors of a third, but that possibility had never been officially documented. Jarvan left no inheritance for either wife or for his four children in Greenville, Mississippi, or for the two in Jacksonville. Jarvan had, when occasionally employed earlier, been a truck driver, absent from home for lengthy periods of time.

Left to navigate the tumultuous journey of motherhood alone, Emily faced a future fraught with obstacles and uncertainties. Horatio's entrance into the world was, obviously, not without its challenges. Adding another layer to their story, Emily and Horatio were not only bound by their familial ties but also by the unique circumstances of their environment. As Caucasians in a predominantly black neighborhood, they stood out amidst the sea of darker faces that populated their community. Their presence, a rarity in the vibrant tapestry of South Chicago, served as a constant reminder of the artificial, but nevertheless real, divisions that existed within their society.

Despite the challenges that lay ahead, Emily held her newborn son close, her love for him a beacon of hope amidst the poverty that surrounded them. Together, mother and child embarked on a journey filled with trials and triumphs, their bond serving as a testament to the resilience of the human spirit in the face of adversity.

CHAPTER 2

ANCHOR IN THE STORM

Emily's decision to work part-time stemmed from her desire to be as present as possible in her son's life. Sure, she knew she'd be eligible for welfare, but that was not the stuff of which she was made. Furthermore, she was quite aware of the apparent hopelessness that people experienced when they depended totally upon government largesse. Knowing the importance of early childhood development and wanting to provide Horatio with the care and attention he deserved, she made sacrifices to ensure he was well looked after. With her work schedule adjusted to allow her afternoons free, in the mornings Emily entrusted her precious son to the care of a neighbor's 12-year-old daughter, Angelica Winston. Despite the young girl's mental challenges, Emily found solace in Angelica's reliability and genuine care for Horatio. Angelica attended a special school in the afternoons, so schedules aligned themselves nicely. Emily enjoyed helping Angelica to cope with everyday human relationships which often scared the girl.

Emily's days were spent toiling away at the local convenience store, where she greeted customers with a warm smile from 8 AM to noon, six days a week. But her dedication didn't end there. On Friday and Saturday nights, Emily would extend her work hours, serving popcorn to the patrons of the local theater, earning extra income to support her two-person family. Although, legally, the theatre was supposed to close by midnight, more often than not, she didn't get home until 2 AM, eight hours after starting her shifts. Although the establishment made a token effort to close on time, sometimes the movies went on past closing time, and not always because of technical glitches.

Despite the demands of her jobs, Emily sought moments of respite and spiritual nourishment for herself and Horatio. On Sundays, when her weary body allowed, she would take him to church, instilling in him the values of faith and community. However, the harsh realities of their circumstances often intervened. A minimal diet and fatigue from her long work hours on weekend nights often left Emily too exhausted to make the lengthy walk to church. When she was unable to make the journey (sometimes there wasn't enough money for the bus), she would turn on the old flea-market-purchased Sony transistor radio and listen to Moody Radio, call letters WMBI.

Winter presented additional challenges. The biting cold of the Windy City made their trek to church, a 15-block journey, all but impossible. Emily's clothing, worn and threadbare from years of use, offered little protection against the northerly breezes that swept through the streets. Her son's comfort may have been assured with a cozy flannel swaddle blanket, but the frigid wind was often too bitter for Emily. As a result, their attendance at church during the winter months became sporadic, a casualty of their struggle to endure the harsh elements of their environment. Radio WMBI got a good workout during the cold months.

As Horatio grew, Emily recognized the importance of providing him with opportunities for growth and social interaction beyond their small duplex and the confines of their neighborhood. In her quest to offer him a sense of community and belonging, she turned to her church, where the doors were open not only to worship but also to programs that catered to the children and youth of the community.

Thus, at a tender age, Horatio found himself enrolled in the Boys and Girls Clubs hosted by the church. In spring and fall, Horatio happily walked, and, in winter, he often got a ride with neighbors in their "ol' rattletrap" as its owner, kindly LaDwayne Montague (with the blackest face and the biggest smile in the 'hood), lovingly referred to it. These clubs served as a haven for children like him, providing a safe and nurturing environment where they could learn, play, and forge meaningful connections with their peers.

For Horatio, the Boys and Girls Clubs became more than just a place to pass the time; they became a second home—a sanctuary where he could explore his interests, develop his talents, and build friendships that would last a lifetime. Under the guidance of dedicated mentors and volunteers, he engaged in a myriad of activities, from arts and crafts to sports and games, each experience contributing to his personal growth and development.

Through his involvement in these clubs, Horatio not only honed his social skills but also cultivated a sense of responsibility and leadership. He learned the value of teamwork and cooperation, as well as the importance of empathy and understanding in his interactions with others – regardless of skin color. Almost all the children came from poor families, so elitism never entered the picture. Although there were occasions when he was called "Whitey", it was usually said good-naturedly and accompanied with a mischievous smile.

As he participated in various club activities, Horatio's confidence blossomed, and he began to discover his own strengths and interests. Whether he was somewhat awkwardly dribbling a basketball on the court, crafting what only his mother would have called a "masterpiece" in the art room, or simply engaging in lively conversation with his peers, he found a sense of belonging that transcended the boundaries of his sometimes-scary surroundings where crime was not unknown.

For Emily, seeing her son thrive within the nurturing embrace of the Boys and Girls Clubs brought immeasurable joy and relief. Knowing that he was surrounded by caring adults and positive influences, she took solace in the knowledge that he was building a foundation for a bright and promising future.

Through his early attendance at the Boys and Girls Clubs, Horatio not only found a sense of belonging but also forged friendships and memories that would shape the course of his life for years to come. And as he continued to grow and, in his own way, flourish, Emily stood by his side, her unwavering love and support guiding him every step of the way. Much later in life, when speaking to friends and work associates, it was not unusual for Horatio to refer to his mother as "my rock".

Despite Emily's steadfast dedication to Horatio's well-being, their circumstances often dictated a life of scraping by. While they never went seriously hungry, their meals were often meager. Emily's resourcefulness ensured that Horatio's clothes were always mended and clean, even if they were threadbare and worn. Despite the challenges, Emily poured her heart and soul into her son, instilling in him values of respect, empathy, and tolerance.

From a young age, Horatio learned to treat others with respect, regardless of their station in life. Emily emphasized the importance of respecting authority figures such as teachers and law enforcement personnel, as well as showing kindness and understanding towards those who were less fortunate or those who may have treated him unkindly. "We don't know what happened in Clyde's home this morning," would be her typical response to Horatio's sometimes tearful reports. Despite occasional jibes and teasing from his peers, Horatio remained steadfast in his commitment to getting along with everyone, a testament to his mother's teachings.

While school was never a passion for Horatio, Emily did her best to support him academically, despite her own limited education. However, as he progressed through the grades, it became evident that academic success did not come easily to him. Despite Emily's efforts to help him with his homework, Horatio struggled to keep up, often finding himself falling behind his peers.

Similarly, Horatio failed to find his niche in extracurricular activities. His lack of aptitude in academics translated smoothly into a disinterest in sports, where he found himself neither excelling nor enjoying himself. His less-than-powerful build made him an unlikely candidate for football, and his mid-teen lack of coordination drastically hindered his ability to excel in basketball. Nor, did it seem, he could accurately pick up the spin of the baseball when he was up to bat … three strikeouts in four at-bats, combined with the .026 batting average, didn't put him on the first team. His only sports interest was in track but, even there, a finish better than 6th in a 10-person race was rare, regardless of distance. Despite his best efforts, Horatio remained on the sidelines, watching as his peers found success and fulfillment in their respective pursuits. Perceived as his shortcomings, Horatio had opportunity to become depressed and, it must be admitted, occasionally succumbed to the temptation. At times like this, Emily would bake him his favorite dessert, pistachio cake, with its not-too-sweet icing. Of course, she'd always share words of encouragement with him at these times – "We're not all gifted with athletic and intellectual prowess, but we're all gifted with something and, my dear boy, you will discover that you have gifts that are unique to you." Nine times out of 10, this combination of tasty food and a mother's encouragement would bring him out of his gloomy state.

CHAPTER 3

TOGETHER WE STAND

However, amidst the challenges of academics and athletics, a new spark lit a flame in Horatio's life. The flint was triggered in the form of Melody Lacoste, a bright-eyed brunette who captured his attention from the moment she and her parents (Francois "Frankie" and Annabelle Lacoste, Cajuns to the core) arrived from New Orleans. With Melody's arrival, Horatio found himself drawn to her infectious energy and zest for life; his priorities shifted as he sought to navigate the complexities of adolescence and young love. Best of all, he soon discovered that the pretty girl was also attracted to him. His rare episodes of gloom and doom were now more frequently replaced with sunshine and roses.

The intuition of parents, especially mothers, has, from time immemorial, been extremely keen. While Frankie was vaguely aware that his daughter was acting somehow differently than normal, he attributed it to the normal hormonal changes in teenage girls … that 'bailiwick', he thought to himself, was Annabelle's department. On

Annabelle's part, she knew what was going on, but not with whom Melody was enamored.

At the same time, in Emily's case, she also knew that something significant, in terms of the fair sex, was happening in Horatio's life. No longer were there any signs of minor depression on his part. In fact, conversely, "elation" would better have described Horatio's state of being. Not only that but, for some reason, he was paying particular attention to his appearance. Whereas, until recently, she had to remind him to comb his hair before leaving the house, he was now spending historically much more time in the bathroom. He was even "lifting weights" … two iron rods left behind on a vacant lot years ago by some construction crew. One of the short stubby rods weighed about 10 pounds and the other probably 12 or 13. To ensure he wouldn't get too muscular on one side of his body, he'd change the day-to-day routine from one hand to the other.

As the normal course of action dictates, the parents questioned their offspring as to what was going on. Melody quipped, "I met this great guy," and then went on into rapturous detail concerning "the nicest man I've ever met … aside, of course, from you, Dad." Indeed, Melody became quite vociferous in her description of Horatio. Not only did he have a very romantic sounding name, but he treated her so well and, blushing ever so slightly, she effervesced, "I think he loves me!" By the time her parents retired for the night, some two hours later, they had been informed that Horatio was, if not the most handsome, most respectable, most polite young man, he was certainly in the top five in the state of Illinois.

Horatio's response to his mother was not quite as effusive, but nevertheless just as sincere. When questioned teasingly by Emily, Horatio initially tried to change the subject but, when that ploy didn't work, he admitted, "I like this girl." He volunteered little else, but he didn't have to. Emily was able to retire to her nighttime quarters less than 10 minutes later.

The young swain, once the 'secret' was exposed, happily introduced his mother to Melody when they happened to meet at a parent/teacher day. Emily encouraged Melody to ask her parents to come over for coffee and apple pie – behind Emily's duplex a Golden Delicious apple tree had made its home, sometime before her parents had acquired the dwelling.

And so it was that the prospective in-laws met. Almost surprisingly, in response to the initial trepidation of the young people, their parents got along swimmingly right from the start. In fact, they got on so well that Melody and Horatio were able to migrate to a corner where they had their own, more intimate, conversation.

As Horatio's high school graduation approached (Melody was a 16-year-old sophomore and Horatio matriculated a year late at 19), it marked not only a milestone, but also afforded more than a moment of reflection for him. Despite the academic and extracurricular challenges he had faced throughout his school years, he found himself standing on the threshold of adulthood, ready to embark on the next chapter of his life – whatever that might be. The Boys and Girls Clubs had played a significant role in shaping his character and providing him with a sense of belonging, but now it was time to step out into the wider world.

Graduation day was a culmination of years of hard work and perseverance, not just for Horatio, but also for Emily, who had stood by his side through the hurdles they'd experienced together. He received no scholastic or athletic awards (his public school had become a bit of a rarity, not giving everyone an almost meaningless award for 'participation') but as he walked across the stage to receive his diploma, both he and his mother couldn't help but feel a sense of pride and accomplishment, knowing that their combined efforts had overcome numerous challenges to reach this moment. Emily's not-infrequent admonition to him during his high school years, "Whatever you do, Horatio, you must finish high school. It opens all kinds of doors for you." Of course, Melody's congratulatory hug and lingering kiss didn't detract from the joy of the occasion.

Amidst the celebrations and well-wishes from friends, Horatio couldn't shake the feeling of uncertainty that lingered in the back of his mind. While many of his peers seemed eager to dive headfirst into the next chapter of their lives (admittedly, there were a few who couldn't have cared less, saying, "I'm going to live off the fat …"), Horatio felt a sense of apprehension about what the future held for him. "Where will I find work around here? Who will have me? I want to be near Melody. I'm scared" … all very real thoughts and apprehensions that, not infrequently, disturbed waking moments as well as nighttime slumber.

One constant source of comfort and stability amidst the uncertainty was his relationship with Melody. Their bond had grown stronger over time, fueled by shared experiences and a deep, almost spiritual, connection that transcended the challenges they faced individually. Despite the occasional bumps in the road, they were weathering the little tempests of youth together, emerging stronger and more committed to each other. Even though they'd known each other for a relatively short time, the connection was real, eclipsing mere physical attraction.

In navigating the ups and downs of young adulthood, Horatio and Melody made the mutual decision to wait until Horatio was 21 before considering marriage. While they were deeply in love and totally committed to each other, they both recognized the importance of using their God-given common sense. Displaying an almost beyond-their-years wisdom, they knew if they married at 19 and 16 1/2, they would "be in tough" if they didn't have a means of livelihood. So, despite their yearning to be together all the time, they made the hard, but ultimately sensible decision. Some of their friends had resorted to common-law relationships even in their mid-teens and, though "H & M" were sometimes teased as "fossils" for their "old fogey morality", they stuck to their convictions. Emily had recounted her life's experiences to Horatio … "I really thought Jarvan would stick with me, but you know what happened," she stated, with a break in her voice and a tear in her eye.

As Horatio embarked on life's post high school journey, he and Melody remained steadfast in their commitment to each other, knowing that their love would continue to grow and evolve with each passing day. And while the road ahead was sure to be filled with challenges and obstacles, they faced the journey with optimism and determination, secure in the knowledge that they had each other's unwavering support and love.

And a journey it was. Horatio had scanned the ads daily prior to his grad, but now his scanning turned into studious examination. There were very few jobs available and none for which he felt capable. There was no point in applying to the ad for a physics teacher in Lincoln Park. Another advertisement for "sewage technician", despite its promise of high pay ("up to $12.50 per hour"), for some reason, had a certain lack of appeal for him. A further highlighted bulletin proclaimed the need for a window washer for downtown Chicago skyscrapers. Somehow, working on the outside of the 110-storey Sears Tower had little appeal to someone who feared getting up on the ladder to clean the gutters on the eaves of a two-story duplex. However, he knew he was reliable, methodical, and had no desire to 'slouch' his way through a workday.

So, the search began. Then, one cloudy wet day in late June, he trudged 19 blocks to a distant garage, then 5 blocks north to a warehouse (where he spent 15 minutes with the very pleasant human resources man who wondered, "You remind me of someone"), and then back home where he stopped at a bakery (he'd done enough baking with his Mom and had enjoyed it) … everywhere he was responded to with "I wish I had something for you" and similar sentiments; he disconsolately weaved his way home. He had only one boot off when the phone rang. At the other end of the line was a totally unexpected call from his high school principal, Mr. Joseph Radner, bearing news that would alter the course of Horatio's immediate future and, ultimately, his life.

"Whitt Whittaker, our assistant janitor, was in a bad accident yesterday. He is in intensive care in South Shore Hospital and won't be able to get back to work for a long time, if ever. Would you be interested in working with the head caretaker? I've talked to Benjamin Carmichael, and he'd love for you to work with him. Mr. Carmichael told me this morning about how he had been watching you during your high school years – always staying back after events to stack chairs, volunteering for various cleanup jobs, and just being what your fellow students called you – 'a neatnik'. He'd like you to come in tomorrow so that he can show you the ropes and get you started. And, Horatio, please be aware that, at least initially, this would be referred to as a 'temporary' job." Working as an assistant janitor would not be remotely associated with the prestige of a doctor or lawyer, but that reality hardly entered Horatio's mind. It was a lifeline – a chance to earn a livelihood and build up some equity for establishing a home. With a mixture of gratitude and trepidation, Horatio immediately accepted the offer, recognizing the opportunity for the stability and financial security it provided.

Meanwhile, Melody's family had lived in a rented house since their arrival in the community … out of the blue it was sold; even though they'd been told this might happen, it was still a shock. They were forced to relocate to an area almost 10 miles distant. The distance posed a significant challenge for Horatio and Melody's maturing relationship, adding another layer of complexity to their lives. He could get there by bus, but doing so would involve three transfers and would take over 90 minutes to get near to his destination – even then he would have to walk the remaining four blocks. "I need a car … we have to be able to see one another." Although his immediate prospect for employment was realized, yet again his midnight slumbers were disturbed by this new challenge.

Despite Horatio's aptitude for mechanical tasks and his willingness to work on an old car, his heart longed for something far more precious than the fun of working with mere machinery: time with Melody. The prospect of spending countless hours tinkering under the hood of a car in need of constant maintenance paled in comparison to the joy he found in her company. Nevertheless, practicality dictated that he address the pressing need for transportation to bridge the gap between their distant homes.

As he contemplated the type of car he needed, Horatio set his sights on a vehicle that met two essential criteria: it had to be in decent condition, ensuring reliability for the occasional commute to see his dearly beloved; and it had to be affordable within his constrained budget. In his recent visit to the neighborhood clinic after he'd cut himself while cleaning up some broken glass, he had seen a "Car and Driver" magazine featuring BMWs and Audis. The dream of such luxury brands remained exactly that—a dream—as he reckoned with the reality of his financial constraints.

With a job offer promising $14.00 per hour, Horatio embarked on a careful calculation of his potential earnings. Factoring in the inevitable deductions, he estimated that he would be left with approximately $90 per day or $450 per week. While this income provided a modest foundation, it fell short of the price tag associated with even most economy vehicles. A 10-year-old sedan with low mileage would probably be affordable.

The day following the principal's call Horatio met with the head caretaker and was reassured of the initial $14/hour, but was also informed that, should he prove satisfactory, he could expect 3% annual raises. If he had to work overtime, he would get paid time and a half.

With Melody's unreserved encouragement and willingness to sacrifice a few days apart, he began scouring listings for reliable used cars that fit his budget. Each potential purchase was subjected to rigorous scrutiny, weighing the balance between affordability and quality. He avoided one obvious scam … the seller wanted a $500 down payment in advance for a car that didn't exist. He also, thankfully, missed out on "a very low mileage '78 Gremlin" which the owner promised he'd bring over to Horatio's home. Neither the car nor the driver showed up. When Horatio sought the reason for the no-show, the fellow's mother admitted the car had broken down two blocks from home.

In the end, Horatio's pragmatic approach led him to a modest yet (reputedly) dependable 8-year-old Chevy that met his needs without breaking the bank. On taking it for a test drive and having a local mechanic friend look at it, his decision was made. He couldn't help but think of Rory Janvier, the good-looking all-around athletic jock who had put down $200, borrowed $8000, then lost his job in his uncle's machine shop due to consistently showing up late. Having the repo man come to take away Rory's pride and joy, a 12-year-old Corvette, had brought down significantly the esteem in which the cheerleaders had held him. Horatio did have to go to the bank for the balance of $2200 after he had made a substantial down payment of $1900 he'd saved up through the years of delivering the Tribune and mowing lawns. His "new" car was hardly a flashy symbol of wealth and status, but it represented a tangible step towards greater independence and accessibility, allowing him to reliably traverse the distance between himself and the young lady he loved. The occasional "Get a horse" and "Did that used to be a car?" didn't faze him. He saw the humor in the jibes, but also had his long-term view in mind.

And so, armed with determination and a newfound sense of purpose, Horatio knew that the true value lay not in the brand or price tag, but in the memories and moments he would share with Melody along the way. If his heart could sing, it would have been playing its own 'melody'. Horatio then embarked on his first car trip to Melody's house. Meanwhile, his sweetheart, knowing Horatio was looking for a car, but not knowing that he had purchased one, heaped successive praises on his good choice. In token of her esteem, she also used the opportunity to bestow similarly successive displays of affection on the owner of the car. Her genuine admiration for his choice of car only served to deepen Horatio's sense of contentment, reinforcing his belief that true happiness lay not in material possessions, but in the love and appreciation of those closest to him. Horatio could not have felt better if the car had been a Lamborghini. Both young people realized that this tangible symbol of independence represented a significant milestone in their combined journey toward adulthood. Horatio's choice of vehicle turned out to be 'a setting of precedent' for subsequent financial decisions.

Later that evening, with Melody's parents discreetly moving to the living room, Horatio and Melody sat down at the kitchen table to do some serious planning. By this time, although not formally engaged, both knew it would be just a matter of time. Because of his "Chevrolet" (he liked to call the car by its rightful name, emphasizing the last syllable), Horatio had still been on a high, but Melody (ever practical) suggested that they get down to a more mundane level to discuss their future.

Taking that practical approach to financial planning, they delved into discussions about their immediate and long-term goals. Horatio's steady income, supplemented by overtime hours, would provide a solid foundation for their future endeavors. With a disciplined approach to saving, they earmarked a portion of their income for both short-term needs and long-term aspirations, including the eventual purchase of a home and even the far-off need for retirement income.

By diligently setting aside 10% of his take-home pay and earning a modest 3% interest on his savings, they realized that, in 16 years (hopefully less), Horatio would steadily have accumulated the funds necessary to transition from renting to home ownership. With a house appreciating in value, even if only 3% per year, their investment in home ownership promised to provide long-term stability and financial security for what they hoped would be their growing family.

In addition to their savings plans, Horatio and Melody also discussed taking advantage of available tax planning strategies, including contributions to an Individual Retirement Account to maximize their savings and minimize their tax liabilities. Through careful planning, they laid the groundwork for a future filled with promise and opportunity, secure in the knowledge that their love and commitment would see them through whatever challenges lay ahead. Following this hour-and-a-half discussion, they generously thanked one another with a token of affection which, incidentally, Melody's Dad commented on when he saw the edge of Horatio's mouth as Melody's beau was taking his leave. For some reason, Melody and her mother were giggling.

Both Melody and Horatio had grown up in homes where the parents had been judicious in their choices. That attitude had rubbed off on both. Horatio had watched his mother scrimp and save as long as he could remember; yet Emily was rarely seen without a smile on her face and joy in her heart. His appreciation of his loving mother exhibited itself by his looking after many of the inevitable equipment breakdowns and other, more minor, eventualities that happen in every household. He knew he would have to live at home for at least a while longer, so he willingly "pulled his weight" around the little dwelling. Their lawn was smaller than many of the ones he had mowed with fuel-powered mowers throughout his teen years, and here at home he used the old push mower that Emily had inherited from her parents. Horatio recognized the sacrifices Emily had made on his behalf, and he did all he could to make her busy life a little easier. Of course, by the time Horatio was 10 or 11, Emily began working full time at the convenience store, giving up her late Saturday night stints at the theatre.

As Horatio reflected on his journey through high school and the challenges he had faced, he couldn't help but recall a lesson from his "Social Awareness" class during 12th grade (the teacher had objected to "Social Studies" as the word "awareness" was, as she called it, "more in-your-face"). The topic of discussion in this somewhat unfocused class ended up being the findings of the Brookings Institute, which purported that young poverty-line Americans had a better than 84 percent chance of entering the middle class if they focused on three key factors. His teacher, Lola Vang, newly out of some college way out west, had almost angrily mocked these findings when one of the brighter lights in the class, Jesse Ewbank, had cited this Brookings study (Jesse's mother worked in a law office). Ms. Vang had categorically stated that those findings were skewed by the rich and privileged crowd. "You can rarely, if ever, get out of the cycle of poverty." She had then gone on with one of her favorite rants about how no one should make $10,000 a year more than anyone else. "If the billionaires would share their money, no one would have to be poor!" she proclaimed with little evidence, but with great conviction. Incidentally, Lola Vang's tenure at the school came to an abrupt end after her inaugural year. Unfortunately, she and the business teacher, Kevin Martinez, did not get along. The high-pitched voice of Ms. Vang haranguing the quiet Mr. Martinez, sometimes even before classes were dismissed, was a bit too much for the administrators to stomach on an ongoing basis. Thus, with the best wishes of the school district, Ms. Vang was given the next year off. To Ms. Vang, this was just another incontrovertible proof of how the poor would always stay poor.

The first of these Brookings findings, Horatio recalled, was to finish high school, regardless of the quality of instruction. Horatio recognized the significance of this advice, understanding that a high school diploma served as a foundational step towards securing stable employment and laying the groundwork for future opportunities. Despite the academic struggles he'd faced, Horatio had persevered, knowing that completing high school was essential to achieving his long-term goals.

The second factor emphasized by the Brookings Institute was the importance of obtaining a full-time job. As Horatio navigated the challenges of post-graduation employment, he realized the significance of this advice firsthand. The opportunity to work full-time not only provided him with a source of income but also instilled a sense of responsibility and independence.

The third and final factor highlighted by the Brookings Institute was the recommendation to wait until at least 21 to get married and have children. While this advice may have seemed arbitrary to some (given the tendency to cohabitation by many in their teens), Horatio understood the rationale behind it. By delaying marriage and not starting a family until later in life, young adults could focus on establishing themselves vocationally and financially, thereby increasing their chances of long-term success and stability.

As Horatio reflected on these three key factors, he realized that they aligned closely with his own experiences and aspirations. Despite the personal obstacles he faced along the way, he remained steadfast in his commitment to achieving his goals and building a better future for himself and his dearly loved Melody. And, as he continued on his life's journey, he carried with him (despite Ms. Vang's near apoplectic fuming) the valuable lessons imparted by the Brookings Institute, knowing that they would serve as guiding principles for years to come ... years that, he knew, would involve Melody.

CHAPTER 4

THE PROPOSAL

It was time.

Feeling certain that Melody would say yes to a proposal of marriage, Horatio went to work with purpose and zeal. It was not long before Mr. Carmichael informed Principal Radner that the school was benefiting more than was Horatio. He related three examples, two of which represented Horatio's foresight, and another in which Horatio's quick action prevented a minor disaster. He recommended that Horatio be given a Christmas bonus that year. The young man was working until the job was done, even if it meant that he was laboring overtime without claiming overtime pay. When reminded of that oversight, Horatio replied, "I know I worked longer, but everyone was having such a good time after the concert, I just waited around until they left. It's no big deal." Even the students appreciated Horatio's efforts. Rather than scolding and becoming upset when a senior student (named Emmanuel Irvine but preferring his self-imposed nickname "Manly") absentmindedly tossed a candy wrapper on the hall floor, Horatio kindly asked Manly to make an effort to keep the hallways looking clean for everyone. As Horatio picked up the candy wrapper, he heard Colleen Koolidge, a popular junior whose flawless chocolatey skin was admired (and sometimes even envied) by all the girls, say to the group of young people surrounding her, "He's such a nice guy – let's not make extra work for him." The guilty party reddened a bit; he'd had his eyes on "Cool" Colleen for a few weeks now and had hoped to make a good impression on her. Hearing her comment brought him up short. He shrunk within himself, vouchsafing in no uncertain terms, "I won't do that again!"

Horatio flourished in his work. Administrators, teachers, and students alike noticed that Horatio was rarely seen without a smile on his face. Although, like a prairie wildfire, the word got around the school that Horatio was in love, his consistent good-natured attitude was evident regardless of whether he was placing chairs for the high school musical or if he was up to his elbows in toilet bowls. He seemed always to have a kind word to say to everyone. And, if it was necessary to warn a student about his or her actions, it was always with an attitude that was universally understood as, "I was your age not that long ago myself!"

Time went by, as it always does, and before they knew it, Horatio and Melody had been a serious item for almost 2 years. Horatio was 21. In addition to making his car payments on time (and he was almost done with them), Horatio had succeeded in setting aside enough money for an engagement ring. Admittedly, it was not the Hope diamond, but it did have a tiny sparkler that he was sure would put a reflecting glow in Melody's eyes. Then, one warm June evening without a breath of wind, he picked Melody up. When she asked where they were going to go that evening, he simply, with a secretive smile, offered, "It's a surprise."

With question marks in Melody's eyes and a knowing smile on Horatio's face, they soon found themselves in Steelworkers Park. The former US Steel site had been transformed with walking paths and lovely views of Lake Michigan. With their arms around each other's waists, they strolled along, enjoying the landscaped lawns and flower beds. They approached a somewhat secluded area nestled in amongst some towering oak trees. The squirrels were chattering above them, but the young couple was oblivious, lost in the world of young love. Upon arriving at a bench, Horatio suggested they sit down and rest for a while. This they did. Question marks still floated around in Melody's eyes, but as Horatio looked deeply into those pools of promise, he also sensed happy suspicion in them.

For a few minutes they spoke of how beautiful it was to be here. But Horatio couldn't wait any longer. Arising from the bench, he got down on one knee and, out of his back pocket, he brought out a small rectangular wrapped package. Of course, every girl intuitively knows what these packages contain, but still coyly asks, "What is it?" And, like every other young man from time immemorial, Horatio, heart pounding, simply suggested, "Open it." Since the reader already knows what passed between the two, further information is deemed unnecessary concerning the hugs and kisses that followed. Even the squirrels seem to be raising the decibel level of their chirping. Excitement reigned. Creation rejoiced.

It was June 26. The drive back to Melody's home was like no other.

CHAPTER 5

AFTERMATH

June 27 dawned sunnier and brighter than either Horatio or Melody had imagined possible. Horatio went about his janitorial duties at the school as if in a trance. In terms of his productivity, that day was probably the least efficient of his short career in that capacity. Mr. Carmichael, having been informed that Horatio had "ringed his girl" last night, did not even reprimand Horatio for his absentmindedness. The head custodian couldn't help but smile – he remembered his own actions the day after his engagement to Edith. His smile broadened as he continued to watch Horatio from a distance. His understudy was seen to grab a mop and pail, ostensibly to clean up an accidental soda can spill. Then he saw Horatio walking past the water tap, carrying the empty pail down the hallway. It was only when he got to the spill that Horatio realized he had forgotten the water. Setting the pail down on the floor and grabbing the mop, he headed back to the supply room to get the water. Arriving at his destination, he realized he was without the pail. The rest of the day didn't go much better.

As for Melody, although she was, understatedly, in high spirits, the evidence of her joy was illustrated by her almost nonstop singing throughout the day. Her parents had been informed of the good news by a note that Melody had left on the kitchen table the night before. Next morning, after the hugs and sincere words of congratulation from Francois and Annabelle, Melody began singing. In itself, that was not so unusual … she often hummed or sang a little phrase or two from a popular hit song she'd heard on the family's ancient transistor radio or a hymn she'd learned in church. She'd always had a good voice and had been asked, from time to time, to sing at school and, on occasion, even in church. However, today her voice seemed to have noticeably more quality than her mother had ever heard. Melody seemed to hit the high notes effortlessly and, when she attempted Karen Carpenter's "Top of the World", her mother had never heard Melody hit those low notes so exquisitely.

The next evening Horatio was again at Melody's door. This was a major departure from his usual once or twice-a-week visits. "I just couldn't wait to see ..." But before he could complete the obvious ensuing words, Melody had smothered his mouth with the affectionate kisses of a newly engaged young lady. Although, that afternoon, the day had suddenly turned cloudy, rainy, and unseasonably cool, the evening's efforts to dampen their spirits went unheeded.

After further displays of affection (which we need not go into here), almost in unison … "When are we going to get married?" After laughing and commenting on how they were already thinking alike, they got down to practical details which, although less romantic than events immediately preceding them, were now becoming essential. Melody's mother "happened" to come into the kitchen at that moment, indicating she'd like to bake some gingersnap cookies. For some reason known only to mothers of brides-to-be, the gingerbread cookies were forgotten as she sat down at the table with them and, together, the three of them laid out wedding plans! Francois remained glued to his White Sox game on TV.

Horatio and Melody decided that the wedding should occur one year from today – one year from today would be a Saturday. From that point, mother and daughter monopolized the conversation. Melody would wear her mother's wedding dress. For a considerable space of time they talked about adding this and adjusting that, having to do some work on the veil and, oh yes, somehow lengthening the dress a touch (Melody was 4 inches taller than her mother). As Horatio was increasingly left out of the conversation, he smiled benignly as mother and daughter spoke of the myriad details that are of little, or no, import to grooms of any era. He migrated to the living room where Frankie was watching the game. "I knew you'd be joining me shortly," he chuckled.

Of course, whether a singer nails that high note or whether a climber successfully reaches the mountain summit, neither can remain at those heights. Both must descend to base camp where more mundane activities await those who have achieved their dreams.

The months seemed to come and go in a blur for the young couple, especially for Horatio. Fortunately, the succeeding days featured little or none of the ineptitude displayed by him on the day following his engagement. Needless to say, the events of "that day" provided Mr. Carmichael with plenty of opportunity to tease Horatio, both personally and publicly, as well as providing Horatio with plenty of opportunities to exhibit his best shamefaced smile. On the other hand, Melody and her mother were coping very well with the myriad wedding plans. The church was booked for the wedding, the pastor agreed to officiate as well as to provide a number of pre-wedding consultations. It would be a small wedding – affordability was at a premium – and the reception for about 30 people would be held in the basement of the church. Both happy mothers agreed to look after most of the meal arrangements. The ladies of the church agreed to help with a few salads and desserts. Horatio's only input into the meal was, "Make sure the dessert is pistachio cake!" Annabelle would prepare the Cajun ham roast and Emily would prepare the mashed potatoes, the veggies, and a couple of 25-pound turkeys with all the trimmings.

CHAPTER 6

NUPTIAL PRELIMINARIES

Now that Horatio had a car, he added regular church attendance to his routine. Emily was so proud of her son and gladly accompanied him, even on chilly winter mornings. Of course, once there, Horatio and Emily usually parted ways as Horatio awaited the arrival of Melody and her parents. Their pastor, Rev. Wilfred Williams (who made a point of asking his parishioners to call him either "Pastor Wilf" or just "Wilf"), having promised to provide premarital counseling for the young couple, took a special interest in them. He was a man of about 40, strongly built, and was a truly imposing figure. He'd been raised in Alabama, graduated from an all-black high school and been a star linebacker in Division 2 of the NCAA. Not only that, but he had even been scouted by both the Bears and the Jaguars. The Cowboys, too, had invited him to a training camp which they'd hosted in Indianapolis. Instead, Rev. Williams had chosen to go to seminary. Upon graduation, he had received pastoral invitations from two middle class churches in Forest Park and even one from far-away Dallas. When people asked him about his coming to much poorer South Chicago, he smiled, accentuating the outlines of his handsome dark face, and simply observed, "I believe this is where I'm supposed to be." Their little nondenominational church was bursting at the seams. Everyone seemed to know that Pastor Wilf really cared for them.

It did not take long for Horatio and Melody to realize that Pastor Wilfred (as they respectfully called him) truly cared for them as well. Upon learning of their engagement, he immediately set about providing choices of dates for the young couple to receive premarital counselling. They agreed that Friday evenings would be the best time for these meetings. There'd be a minimum of five meetings but, if the situation warranted, there could be more sessions. Any additional meetings beyond the five would be based on either the pastor's sense of what more needed to be shared or upon additional questions that the young couple might seek to have addressed.

The first such meeting was scheduled for early in September. Although both young people felt comfortable with the pastor when there were other people around, they were each a touch nervous as they rang the doorbell of the church. When the part-time secretary buzzed the door open for them, they were only too happy to get out of the oppressive late summer heat. The humidity was rolling in on waves from the great lake that washed the shores of the city. Expecting to be accompanied by the secretary to the pastor's office, they were surprised when, a moment later, the man himself appeared to greet them. He escorted them to his office, offered them coffee, and Melody, nervously giggling, "We're too young to drink coffee." Pastor Williams smiled and, eyes twinkling, observed with a chuckle, "Too young to drink coffee, but old enough to marry! Please be totally comfortable with me. I may be 40, and I know I look it, but I still feel pretty young myself." More at ease, they entered his office which, to their surprise, was opulent only in the sense that it had a lot of books crammed onto insubstantial shelves that were bending in their middles. Although everything was neat, the computer with the CRT monitor bespoke the fact that the pastor was not a spendthrift.

Although, by now, Melody was very much at ease, Horatio felt it incumbent upon himself to discuss the weather. After the pastor agreed with Horatio that, indeed, it was very humid and hot today, he deftly segued into an overview of what they would discuss over the next five or more sessions. Horatio and Melody, just last night, had wondered what topics the pastor would cover. "He'll probably instruct us on how we need to read the Bible and pray every day," was Melody's opinion. Horatio was quick to suggest, "I think the pastor is going to talk to us about how to keep the love light burning! He may even get into more intimate details." With that comment, Melody blushed slightly while squeezing the hand of her betrothed.

Instead of launching into specifics, the pastor gave them a fascinating overview regarding important topics of which they were vaguely aware, but to which they hadn't given specific attention. "There are seven areas of life that I like to call 'The Seven Pillars', each of which contributes to a strong foundation for your future. We will be touching on each of these in one form or another as we meet. Right now, though – I see you've got your notebooks with you – I'm going to list them for you, and briefly mention what is included with each of these pillars."

Pastor Wilfred paused briefly, as if collecting his thoughts, and then, without consulting any notes, began.

"The first vital pillar of life is wisdom. Wisdom obviously addresses your spirituality and how your beliefs will affect your actions. Wisdom clearly involves not just knowledge, but what you've gained from that knowledge and from life lessons learned along the way. It addresses the issues of life and how you will cope with them. Wisdom addresses not only how you will conduct your lives in the brief time allotted to each of us, but it will also address the legacy you wish to leave when you are gone from this earth's scene."

The pastor deliberately paused, himself thinking seriously of the words he'd just uttered, and giving the young couple an opportunity to do the same.

"Pillar #2 is values. Of course, values are very closely related to wisdom. Values involve choices, principles or rules you live by, as well as both short- and long-term priorities.

Another, very important pillar - #3 - supporting the structure of your lives, is finance. Finance involves everything ranging from daily living, dealing with liabilities, planning for the future – including the financial legacy you will leave when you pass away.

All of these pillars of life are intrinsically valuable to a productive and enjoyable life experience. Pillar number 4 is family. Not only are spouse and kids involved, but also all the others who are close to you by birth and marriage. Family involves not only relationships with each other, but also mundane things like storage and organization of documents, and the administration of daily events, both planned and unexpected. Again, the idea of legacy considerations is part and parcel of the family 'pillar'.

Pillar 5 is health. Life is unpredictable – while there are many ways by which we can keep ourselves fit by avoiding harmful practices and by engaging in healthy exercise programs – but, as the old saying goes, 'born to perish, each moment a gift'. Keep accurate records of your medical histories, your doctors, your prescriptions, as well as your health insurance documentation.

The sixth pillar is career. We all need to start somewhere, but give serious consideration, not only to a primary job, but also to concepts and ideas of other things you may be gifted and/or inclined to do. Most people do not stay with the same work their entire lives. There is nothing wrong with doing so, but you may wish to fulfill a dream that will require continuing education. Remember, a career is what provides the finances to strengthen the other pillars!

The seventh, and last pillar I'm going to mention is that of community. How are you going to contribute to the world around you? How will you address the issues that come up in your neighborhood, your state, and your country? Be sure you know the 'influentials' who have the power to make changes." Almost as an afterthought, Pastor Wilf mused, "Remember, though, not to fawn over the rich and famous.

They're sometimes the neediest for the things that really matter." This seventh pillar relates also to your choice of friends, the service organizations you may wish to join, as well as the faith organizations and charities you may wish to support. Don't ever forget the truly needy all around us.

"Now," he continued, "with this overarching superstructure, let's get down to individual topics." Once again, the eyes of the young people met, and Melody blushed – most becomingly – thought Horatio.

But Pastor Wilfred surprised them both. "Let's begin with finances." He went on to explain that a very high percentage of divorces occur because of financial issues. "At your age, far too many young people think they will live forever, not realizing that decades can go by in the blink of an eye. You need to be working in the present, but always keeping the future in mind. And, because there are two people involved, one person always wants to spend more and the other always wants to spend less. Of course," he elaborated, "it is possible that both spend too much – yet there is always one of the two who spends more than the other. At the other extreme, in which both parties like to save money, there is always one who pinches dollars while the other one pinches pennies."

Since the pastor had been through the process of marriage counseling many times before, he gave his little spiel about how important it was to save money, create a budget, and then, as nearly as possible, stay within that budget. "While you may feel it necessary to live in the basement of one of your parent's homes for the first while, that's not something that will appeal to you in the long term. Besides, your parents have done all they could to help you fly on your own. And I'll let you in on a little secret – they don't want you to live with them longer than absolutely necessary. I advise that you get yourselves a home as soon as you can afford it … you don't have to start with a 5-bedroom mansion," he smiled. "Aim for something basic to start with. Furthermore, life goes by very quickly, and when the day comes that you retire, you'll need to have a nest egg to fall back upon. I know that you, Horatio, are good at your work, but I don't imagine you're making $100,000 a year! And you, Melody, have just graduated high school. So, other than for the little spending money that I know you've made by babysitting my darling little 'rug rats' before you moved, and those of others after you left this area, I don't imagine your nest egg is so large that it's going to crack open and spill all over the community."

While the topic of Pastor Wilf's first session with them was a surprise, they were ready for him. Taking turns, they informed him that, by the 15th or 16th year of their marriage, they intended to purchase a modest house. Meanwhile, they'd decided they would look for an apartment. They explained the details of their savings plans and how the loans officer who had provided Horatio's car loan told them, when they'd both visited him, that she wished all her clients would be as conscientious as was Horatio. "If you ever require another loan for any good reason, I won't be asking you a lot of questions!" The pastor then asked them how they would manage financially if and when children came along. Horatio reported that his supervisor at the school, Mr. Whittaker, had told him he intended to take early retirement, as his wife's maiden aunt had left them a substantial inheritance. The head caretaker position would be Horatio's by the middle of the next calendar year. At that time, his salary would be increased by almost 50%. Melody, during her final two years in high school, had shown a real aptitude for consumer math. Her teacher, Mrs. Patricia Golding, having had experience with Windy City Financial Services, an accounting firm, promised she'd put in a good word for her at the agency. She had, in fact, already told Mr. Anthony "Tony" Scrivens, the manager, that she had a promising work candidate in her class. Mrs. Golding hinted that the starting salary would be in the $20 per hour range. Melody told the pastor that she and Horatio had talked about getting financially established before having children. Ideally, she indicated, they'd like to start having children after four or five years.

"Frankly, I'm almost a bit overwhelmed at the thought and, especially at the actions, you have already taken," responded the pastor. "You two would serve as a wonderful case study for all prospective newlyweds. I am truly impressed, and I congratulate you."

"You know, somehow the wisdom you have shown in your financial planning reminds me of an exceptionally popular book by a guy named – I think it was Stanley Thomas – wait a minute, I know I have it in my library." With that, the pastor rose from his noticeably ancient wicker chair, turned around and took the two steps to his library with its sagging shelves. He obviously had his books arranged in a very organized manner as he was able to find what he was looking for in just a few seconds. "Here it is," he observed. "I'm going to give this book to you – it's well worth reading, and even rereading, at least every couple of years. I've read it at least five times. The title may surprise you. Oh, I see my dyslexia has kicked in again. The author's name is Thomas Stanley, not Stanley Thomas. I hope you are not shocked that a pastor is giving you a book with the title, 'The Millionaire Next Door'. The book was given to me by a real-life millionaire. And, no, he has never lived in a so-called high-class neighborhood. In fact, he lives less than 20 blocks from this church. He drives a nice vehicle, but never purchases new, always looking for something around 3 years old in verified good condition. No one would ever know he is a millionaire – he generously gave a copy of this book to every pastor and counselor of whom he was aware, telling them that he hoped the information contained in it would be shared with young people and young couples with whom they came in contact. I'm not going to mention this man's name because he has no desire to be known as the neighborhood's millionaire. He's a very ordinary man. He and his wife of more than 45 years live in a nice, but far from ostentatious, home."

As the pastor sat back in his visibly comfortable chair, he thought for a moment and then observed, "One of the important lessons of life is to learn from those who make mistakes. Surely, it's important to learn from our own mistakes, but it's much wiser to learn from the mistakes of others. For example," he continued, "I know you won't be getting much financial help from your parents in terms of buying a home … I know they can't do so, but even if they could, it wouldn't necessarily be a good idea. And, I know you are both sensible enough not to look forward to buying a home that is beyond your means. In his book,

Thomas – there I did it again – STANLEY recounts many instances of parents placing large downpayments on homes for their children, not realizing that's probably one of the worst things they can do for them. Large homes require large mortgages, large amounts of furniture and other accoutrements, expensive cars sitting in their driveways, and a myriad of other status symbols – none of which even enter the realm of the necessary."

Following a quiet moment of thoughtful contemplation by all three, the pastor continued. "Credit cards are a wonderful convenience, but they can be a ball and chain on any hope for prosperity. If used wisely, the payments being made every month, and – this is important – not buying things impulsively, these pieces of plastic can be useful tools. Never spend first, then wonder where the money will come from later. Spending more than you earn is never a good policy. Oh, another thing that Stanley mentions in his groundbreaking book truly reveals human nature in its less than admirable reality. He indicates that many young couples start life together in the manner of life to which they have become accustomed in their parent's homes. That's a huge mistake. They feel they have to do that to keep up appearances – which is just another sad example of what happens when pride takes over. Even if some people have little to be proud about, they still want others to think highly of them. It's not a new saying, but 'pride always comes before a fall'."

Again, there was a short silence as they all contemplated the wisdom expressed so succinctly in Stanley's book. Then, almost as an afterthought, Pastor Wilf observed, "Yet another thing mentioned in that book is that couples need to stay together. It can be difficult to get through financially rough times, and every marriage counselor knows that financial disagreements can lead to divorce. But there are relatively few millionaires who are paying alimony to previous spouses … most still live with the original spouse with whom they've experienced life with all its highs and lows. I guess Stanley is really saying couples should stick together through thick and thin. In his well-researched book, Stanley also indicates that any extra money – besides what is already budgeted – should be wisely invested. I know you two are already doing that, and I commend you for it."

Pastor Wilfred confirmed with them the date of their next meeting the following month. However, he did not tell them the subject of the next session. "I'm purposely not telling you because I want you to spend time discussing possible topics. You may not be right in terms of guessing the next topic, but you will have discussed a number of other areas that you need to clarify as you prepare for the lifelong commitment of marriage. The more you talk over these things, the better will be your understanding when you discuss those very subjects with me."

In the days that followed, Melody and Horatio did, indeed, discuss a variety of potential topics. When the agreed-upon Friday night arrived, Horatio no longer felt constrained to discuss the weather in any great detail (there was nothing special about it anyway) when they arrived at the pastor's office. The pastor had made them totally comfortable at the previous meeting, so there was no hindrance to getting right into the subject at hand. And the subject at hand this time was the topic of communication and conflict resolution. It was not the theme that the young couple had guessed it might be – they were still thinking it might have something to do with their spiritual lives or maybe even the emotional and intimate characteristics of a good marriage.

Pastor Wilfred began the second session by emphasizing the importance of open, honest, and respectful communication. He highlighted active listening, expressing feelings without blame, and the importance of nonverbal communication. "Sometimes," and it almost sounded like a warning, "nonverbal communication can be more significant, positively or negatively, than actual words." He taught them how to address disagreements constructively, how to recognize the difference between healthy arguments and destructive fights, and the importance of compromise and understanding. "Inevitably, there will be disagreements … that's a given. When you do have 'tiffs', forgive one another, then, as a pastor friend of mine says, 'Build a bridge and get over it.'" He encouraged them to make a habit of discussing their day, their feelings, and any issues that could arise to prevent small problems from becoming larger conflicts. After this session, while enjoying snow cones at the little ice cream bar nearby, they agreed that their pastor had "hit the right nail on the right head".

Session 3 started a little later than they'd hoped. Not only was Horatio required to stay a little later at the school due to a chemical spill in the lab, but when he finally got out of the building, one of his tires was almost flat. Even though he went without his evening meal, they were almost 20 minutes late. Pastor Wilf readily understood their situation and, when Horatio asked for his forgiveness, indicated that no forgiveness was necessary. "These things are all just life's normal bumps and bruises. You will find that some of these bumps and bruises are preparation for much greater challenges. Meeting minor challenges successfully will provide you with the ammunition necessary to cope with the large ones." This third session dealt with roles and expectations. Wilf spoke of traditional versus modern roles. "How do you plan to divide household chores? What are your personal expectations of your partner? How will you support one another emotionally?" He went on to emphasize the need to be flexible and willing to adapt to different roles as circumstances changed which, he stated with emphasis, "They obviously will change if there are career shifts or children arrive on the scene."

Then arrived Session 4. "This evening, my young friends, we will talk about emotional connection and intimacy. Doubtlessly, you will have discussed some of these things, but I'd like to stress some important details that you may, or may not, have dealt with." He encouraged them to cultivate emotional closeness through shared experiences, deep conversations, and mutual support. He provided guidance on maintaining a healthy physical relationship, respecting each other's boundaries, and understanding the importance of consent and mutual satisfaction. He offered practical tips on keeping the romance alive. "When you're with each other every day and every night, the fires of romance can burn low. Make sure that you have regular date nights, exchange thoughtful gestures and use pet names for one another – and don't forget a sense of playfulness and adventure in your relationship."

Session 5 was the last of the prescribed sessions that the pastor had promised them. This time the venue was different … it occurred in the Williams' home. Pastor Wilf spoke of the importance of aligning their long-term goals and creating a shared vision for their future. These dreams and goals could relate to career, travel, personal development, or other life goals. "And," he continued, "don't forget those less fortunate than you. A good rule-of-thumb is to give away 10% of your income to well-researched worthy causes. You'll not only find great personal satisfaction in doing so, but you'll find it will never hurt you financially." He advised the couple to create a written plan outlining their goals for the next five, 10, and even 20 years, including financial goals for family plans, and personal milestones. The final part of this particular session dealt with life's changes. "Change is inevitable," he assured them as they, with rapt attention, hung on his every word. "There can be health issues, deaths in the family, or unexpected financial burdens. It is important to face these challenges as a team."

As, later, they shared pie and coffee (Horatio liked his black, Melody sweetly asked Mrs. Williams if she had decaf) with the pastoral couple, Rev. Wilf reminded them that he'd be available if they had other discussion topics that they'd like to pursue. "Your financial plans are solid and, from what you told me last week, I believe both of you are growing spiritually – continue to do so. Of course, we could talk about parenting and family dynamics, disciplinary approaches, and balancing career and family life. We don't have to do that now, but if you'd like to have guidance in any of those areas, I am here for you. There's also the whole sphere of coping with external pressures that can be experienced from family, work, or societal expectations. In this area, it's important to maintain a united front, facing the challenges together."

Horatio and Melody expressed their personal gratitude to both Rev. and Mrs. Karena "Call me Kari" Williams. In particular, they had appreciated the practical role-playing exercises where they had taken turns expressing their thoughts on various hypothetical scenarios while the other practiced active listening and empathetic responses. Through these exercises, they learned the value of patience, kindness, and the importance of addressing issues calmly and respectfully. They told the pastor that they realized that effective communication would be essential, not just in their marriage, but in all aspects of their lives. The pastor's insights had provided them with valuable tools to navigate potential challenges and strengthen their bond.

As they left that Friday evening, they almost felt sorry that the sessions were over. As they began walking to the car, Melody whirled around, ran up to Kari and gave her a hug. "You will have to be our first visitors when we establish our home!" As she almost skipped back to where Horatio was standing, with a twinkle in his eye, he couldn't help but say to her, "Are you really the same girl who was so shy on our first visit?"

New adventures awaited.

CHAPTER 7

THE DAYS HASTEN BY

Throughout the quickly passing weeks and months, Horatio remained dedicated to his job at the school. His hard work and positive attitude did not go unnoticed. Mr. Carmichael, upon his retirement and true to his word, recommended Horatio for the head caretaker position. This promotion came with a significant pay increase (not the expected 50% hike, but only about 45% due to the declining economy of the previous two years), providing Horatio and Melody with a more secure financial foundation as they prepared to start their life together.

Melody, too, found success in her exciting new role at the accounting firm. Mrs. Golding's recommendation had opened the door, and Melody's dedication and aptitude quickly made her a valuable asset to the team. Her starting salary of $20 per hour allowed her to contribute significantly to their savings, further solidifying their plans for the future.

With their financial stability growing, Horatio and Melody decided to begin scanning newspapers and the internet for a modest apartment.

While they knew they probably couldn't afford one just now, with the double income, it wouldn't be long. They continued to save diligently, earmarking funds for their eventual home purchase and other long-term goals.

Although they would like to have had more wedding attendants, they settled on just a best man for Horatio and a maid of honor for Melody. Their choices were unique. People talked about their quite unusual selections for months. Horatio had chosen Rory – he of the repossessed Corvette. The soft spot in Horatio's heart ached for Rory's embarrassment and he had expressed his sympathy and concern in such a caring way that Rory had taken a liking to him. They had actually become good friends, somewhat to the bewilderment of the young adults who'd known them in high school. Melody's choice was also quite unique. She chose Angelica as her wedding party companion. Of course, there was quite a difference in age, but Melody had heard so many good stories about Angelica's care for Horatio as he was growing up. Melody had made a point of getting to know Angelica and had much respect for her. Angelica had almost been a second mother to the man who was to become Melody's husband. On being asked, Angelica's joy knew no bounds. Although slightly awkward, she did a somewhat weird happy dance and hugged Melody repeatedly. Seven times, in fact. Horatio had counted.

Almost before they had imagined it possible, their wedding was only days away. The myriad of last-minute details was carefully coordinated by the mothers who, to the immense joy of the young couple, had become great friends.

Then, at long last – and yet so quickly – the big day arrived, bringing with it all the joy and excitement that Horatio and Melody had envisioned. Assisted by Rory (who looked resplendent in his tuxedo) and Angelica (who fairly bubbled with excitement) and surrounded by their closest family and friends, they exchanged vows in a moving ceremony officiated by Pastor Wilfred. Mischievously, the pastor even recounted the now well-known story of Horatio's actions at work following the evening of his engagement. The reception in the church basement was a simple yet beautiful affair, filled with laughter, love, and the warmth of a community that had supported them throughout their journey. Because of the generosity of Melody's parents, they were able to host 10 more guests than they had originally envisioned.

When the festivities finally ended around 11 PM, Horatio shed his wedding jacket and began stacking chairs – cleanup was in his nature, a habit that he found hard to shed even on his wedding day. Pastor Williams, seeing what was happening, strode over to Horatio with the determined walk. "Son, get yourself and your bride out of here - NOW!" The young couple had planned to take their now much-decorated "ChevroLET" to Melody's parent's (their soon-to-be home) to spend their wedding night in the basement. Pastor Williams, however, together with the board of the church, had raised enough money to give the young couple two nights in the Lakefront Luxury Lodge on the lakeshore. Not only that, but Pastor Williams had told his rather well-heeled brother Darrell (who was 17 years younger than himself and playing AAA baseball), about this special young couple. On hearing the story, Darrell had sprung for a limousine ride to the hotel, and back home later. Overwhelmed with gratitude, Horatio and Melody repeatedly offered their thanks. In fact, Melody was seen more than once dabbing wetness from just below her eyes. One of the guests announced, "The limo is here!" Then, in luxury they had never even imagined, the smooth ride to the hotel began – all they could hear were their love whispers one to the other. As the limousine eased onto what some people termed the "unholy" pockmarked streets, the late evening pedestrians (not all of whom were bent on fulfilling honorable pursuits) gawked in amazement at the luxurious conveyance. One of the observers, known only as "Iceman", felt more than a momentary panic. Whatever was left of his long-dormant conscience reminded him of a rather significant number of non-disclosed proceeds from certain contractual obligations. He much valued his knees and had little desire to experience months of rehabilitation. When he realized, to his immense relief, that the limo's occupants were taking no notice of him, he decided to reconsider his earlier deliberations about arranging a relocation of his dwelling-place. His grandfather had told him his ancestors came from the South Sahara. The Iceman thought that, just possibly, he might take up with some of his long-lost relatives.

Upon arrival at the hotel, the concierge herself greeted them, took them right past the registration desk, and escorted them up to the honeymoon suite. The young people were struck almost dumb by the opulence of the room. In all their lives, they had never seen such lovely surroundings. The Jacuzzi was the first thing that attracted their attention; in fact, they had to ask what it was. The furnishings were exquisite, mostly done in Queen Anne style except for the massive heart-shaped bed with an ornate canopy. There was a lovely basket of fruit, and another of drinks and various condiments. Horatio was almost bug-eyed, and Melody literally squealed with delight. The concierge had been through this delightful process scores of times, but the next morning she remarked to her husband that she had never run across a young couple who were so appreciative of their surroundings.

The subsequent activities of the night need not be elaborated upon. The conjectures of the reader will probably be accurate.

The concierge had asked them the previous evening what time they would like to have breakfast. "Can't we just go down to the dining room?" asked Horatio. "No," she responded, "breakfast will be brought up to you." And what a breakfast it was. Melody exclaimed, "If I have to eat all that, I'm going to be fat by tonight!" Horatio laughingly responded, "I'll love you anyway!" At that point, he felt a playful jab in his ribs.

When the two glorious days were over and the limousine had given them a ride back "home", they both realized a number of things. Both had known hard work and low-end incomes, saving some, and scrimping more. In the last two days, they'd seen how the wealthy lived. In fact, on two short trips down to the lobby, both times they'd met an expensively attired gentlemen who had greeted them kindly. They had begun conversing, and Horatio had enthused to the man, a Mr. Jacobs, "Isn't this ever a beautiful hotel!" They didn't expect his response, "Ah, my young friends, this is nothing. The Millenium Park Palace and the Skyline Suites were full, and I was told by a somewhat rude receptionist on the phone, "There is always the Lakefront Lux-Lodge if you can stomach it." "Personally," he shared, "I don't mind staying here although I usually stay in something a little more comfortable."

Thus, Horatio and Melody were exposed to another world. They had never really thought of themselves as being poor before, but now they had a deeper understanding of a world totally foreign to them. They may not have overtly realized it, but they had come to a point in their lives at which, not only were their heretofore single lives disrupted most charmingly, but they had to make some serious life decisions. The immediate temptation, of course, was to envy those who were wealthy and could stay in such beautiful places. A young couple with lesser understanding may well have dejectedly intoned, "We'll never get there." That first evening spent under more austere conditions was spent in a heart-to-heart talk – prior to other, more enjoyable, events taking place.

The first mental decision they had to make was, at all costs, to avoid envying those who had more. They realized the futility of such a negative exercise. Besides, they had but a foggy idea of how people achieved the level of income that afforded them such luxury. Some of them, they correctly realized, had been born into money. Others, they knew, just as deliberately, had chosen, sometimes at great personal expense, to start a business from scratch. In fact, they both knew a now middle-aged man, one Howard Goodman, who had grown up nearby, struggled mightily in establishing a profitable laundromat only three blocks from where Horatio and his mother lived. This man had worked hard, sometimes fixing his own washers and dryers, but within 10 years (at age 30), he had established two more such laundromats. Business had been good, and he'd been able to hire reliable managers; his laundromats were always clean, and profits continued to accumulate. With those extra profits invested, Goodman now owned a chain of 15 laundromats, and he was still only in his mid-40s. By this time he had already invested in one or two other enterprises, helping other young entrepreneurs on their way to potential success. Not only that, but he was known to be a generous philanthropist. Melody and Horatio had met him several times and he'd encouraged them to just "do your best, don't spend wildly, always set money aside for a rainy day and/or retirement, but don't hold back when it comes to helping the truly unfortunate … and don't forget to give yourselves the occasional treat." The young couple understood that, no, not everyone was born into wealth. There were those, like Mr. Goodman, who had been born into abject circumstances, but had worked hard to get where he was. And, no, they certainly couldn't fault him for taking an occasional cruise and a visit to far-off places – and even for staying in expensive hotels if he so chose.

They continued communicating, not only that evening (they also had other things on their minds), but as well on succeeding days when their work was over, and the supper dishes had been put away. Ideas were shared as to how they might position themselves in life in such a way that, when it came to retirement (which was ages and ages in the future) it would certainly be nice to be able to do some of the things that they'd like to do. "Wouldn't it be nice to be able to go to a White Sox game once in a while?" "Can you imagine going on a cruise to Alaska?" "Wouldn't it be wonderful to buy a new sound system for the church?" "Wouldn't it be good to be able to buy a new industrial dishwasher for Pacific Garden Mission?" "Wouldn't it be nice, when our parents get to that age where they are less able to look after themselves, to be able to lodge them in a beautiful assisted-living environment?"

While Melody realized that she and Horatio had already made some logical plans for a stable financial future, it was now time to get serious about making joint plans for a lifetime together, plans which would have to be reviewed regularly. The basics were there, but now they had to get specific. Both the Lacostes and Horatio's mother would, inevitably, be experiencing their own life changes.

CHAPTER 8

LIFE IN THE MARRIED LANE

Two lives had become one. Hydrogen is a flammable gas. Oxygen supports combustion. United, they become water, a life giver to virtually every living creature. Pastor Williams had shared this example with them. He had also provided another example. "This is an instance of which I know personally. Two young adults, Alice and Bob, one in California and one in Arkansas – Alice was a brilliant software developer but had dismal sales for her product because of ineffective marketing. Bob had taken marketing courses in university, had an intuitive aptitude for marketing, and could well have instructed his professors – he was always one step ahead of them. Unfortunately, Bob had nothing to sell. Through the auspices of an online organization, 'Linked-In', built for the purpose, Alice and Bob met. After attaining an in-depth understanding of their respective talents and abilities, they combined their efforts into a forward-looking software organization they called '2Morrow'. Together they became the owners of a wildly successful small company." Pastor Wilfred had then gone on to further state, "That's the way it is with you two. Not only are you combining

49

your lives – becoming 'one flesh' as the good book says – but you are also combining your individual areas of expertise. Horatio, I've heard people refer to you teasingly as a sanitation engineer. While they say it in fun, there is a lot of truth to that description. In fact, a top-level janitor, it could be argued, is one of the most important people in any building, be it a school, a church, a factory, or a high-rise office building. In fact, it could legitimately be argued that a good janitor prevents more illness than a good doctor. And in your case, Melody, you are rapidly learning the ins and outs of the accounting business. Who knows what the combination of those individual activities could hold for the future? That synergy may one day even lead to the possibility of starting a business of your own. Whether you do so or don't do so, no matter what you do, you are stronger together."

As they embarked on their married life, having agreed – temporarily – to live in the basement of Melody's parents' home, they realized how fortunate they were to have had great advice and mentoring, not only from Pastor Williams, but also from their parents. Other changes were happening as well. Emily Jefferson was beginning to see a fine 'mixed race' man about two years her junior, Brad Parnell by name. Brad was a fireman and paramedic and lived in a one-person bachelor apartment about 24 miles southeast of Chicago's South Loop. Even before he'd met Emily, he was hoping to find a place much closer to work. By now there was already some good-natured teasing going on in the close-knit community. Because Emily's duplex was so very small and, should she get married, there would not be room for two couples. On the other hand, while the Lacostes had more room, Melody's father made it clear that, while the young marrieds were welcome to stay for up to six months, after that they would be on what he smilingly called "borrowed time". Horatio had no trouble grasping the intent of his father-in-law. Nor did he even want to burden his in-laws with their extended presence. He readily agreed that he and Melody would begin looking for a place right after his appointment to the head janitorial job. "I know you will, Son, and please understand that you have our blessing in all your efforts. Melody has a good man!" were the welcome words of his father-in-law. "Thanks, Dad."

CHAPTER 9

REPLACEMENT AND RECRUITMENT

Horatio's duties at the school, although totally understood and diligently executed, took on new meaning for him as he looked to the future. He watched his soon-to-be-leaving supervisor closely so that he could more fully understand the responsibilities that would soon be his. He realized that Mr. Carmichael did more than just clean windows and whiteboards. He had also to deal with personnel issues. Not only was there a head custodian and an assistant, but there were also two full-time and three part-time sweepers to supervise as well as service people to call and negotiate with when the need arose.

True to his word, Mr. Carmichael exercised his option to take early retirement and, without any break in the schedule, Horatio would take over the full-time head caretaker position. Well before that appointment was official, Mr. Carmichael had advertised for the position that Horatio was about to vacate. Carmichael asked Horatio to be part of the interview process, an activity which was totally foreign to him. But he found that he enjoyed meeting the five applicants for the position he was leaving.

Horatio and his boss quickly realized that the first of their interviewees, a 38-year-old guy with a scruffy beard and unkempt Afro hairdo whose given name was Harriman Bumblethwaite … ("But just call me 'Astral' because my online name is Astral Artichoke") … would probably not be a good fit. Harriman, thus having, with apparent reluctance, introduced himself, raised one eyebrow … as if raising both would have been an unnecessary bother … muttered something about applying only because his parents wanted him out of the house; they'd told him, in no uncertain terms bordering on vehemence, they had no desire to have an unemployed son live with them throughout their retirement years. Harriman did not share that last snippet of information, but it still rankled him. How could they be so cruel to their own flesh and blood? When Carmichael asked "Astral" what he was doing now, he grunted, "I'm a gamer". Mr. Carmichael asked Harriman if he made money at that job (Carmichael didn't know what a "gamer" was). Harriman croaked, "No, but I do win the occasional bet. It's sort of a break-even activity." The interview ended shortly after that. Very shortly after.

One of the girls who applied, a carefully coiffed and pleasant plain-featured young lady, Maggie Dunbar, made a good first impression on both Mr. Carmichael and Horatio, but that impression was quickly, and negatively, adjusted when she gave nebulous answers to their specific questions while, at the same time, buffing her elongated fingernails with an emery board. Then, in the middle of a question by the head caretaker concerning any previous experience, Maggie interrupted, asking if they had access to a nail clipper. Horatio, with barely concealed sarcasm, suggested she go to the main office and ask the school secretary for manicure supplies. To the amazement of both interviewers, Maggie took Horatio up on his recommendation, popped up like a Jill-in-the-box and, with two bounds covering the nine feet to the doorway, she disappeared. Carmichael, half-chuckling in his astonishment at her hasty departure, commented sardonically, "I wonder how well she did on her high school's track team?" When Maggie, with much anticipation, returned with her clipped and very carefully buffed nail, the interview room was locked. Repeated knocking failed to produce a response.

There was one other female, Serena Blake, who applied. She was a stunningly beautiful 22-year-old blonde Caucasian who would have stood out in any crowd, but especially so in a predominantly black neighborhood. Her mesmerizing green eyes would, without exception, captivate anyone's attention. Their gentle upward curve at the corners added a touch of 'serene' grace. While her work experience was minimal, she did evidence a very good attitude and, without a hint of hesitation, gave clear-cut answers to specific questions. She exuded the strong impression that she was not afraid of diligent work or long hours. After high school, she'd been a caretaker's assistant, working 12-hour days, four days a week, in a personal care home. When asked why she left, without hesitation and smiling confidently, she purred, "I felt it would be more enjoyable working around younger people." Following her departure, Mr. Carmichael asked Horatio, "What did you think of her?" It would've been difficult for any man to have avoided thinking of her (her halter-top added to increasing the level of that difficulty), and Horatio had even dwelt briefly on the idea of how nice it would be to work with such a great-looking young woman. However, she had done something, although very briefly, that had rocketed up a red flag in Horatio's consciousness. During the interview, while Mr. Carmichael's attention had been briefly diverted by a question from Mrs. Rogers, one of the sweepers who'd popped in, this lovely applicant had bestowed a slow wink at him in a manner which couldn't have been interpreted other than in a somewhat 'more than friendly' manner. Horatio, at that very moment, decided that this was not going to work out well. He didn't need that kind of distraction, nor what it could potentially lead to. When he told his boss what had happened, Mr. Carmichael simply concluded, "Well, that sounds dangerous. We'll strike her off the list."

The last two candidates were Bill Withers and Jeff Monahan. There was a very real sense in which they could not have been more different from each other.

Bill was 62 years old and had been retired for two years. He was nearly 6 feet tall, and his tightly coiled kinky hair was just beginning to grey. In the South Chicago neighbourhood, he would have been considered wealthy, having retired after 35 years in the landscaping business. He had been associated with, and was recommended by Urban Oasis Gardens, a popular greenhouse operation. Bill had anticipated his retirement, having worked 12-hour days much of his life, mowing lawns and edging borders in summer, and blowing snow and keeping driveways ice-free in winter. On rainy days, he'd utilized a standing invitation to pop into the local thrift store to fix appliances that had been donated. On those days he worked only 8 hours. He looked forward to "doing nothing" for the rest of his life. To his dismay, "doing nothing" turned out not to be all that it was touted to be. Within the first six months, after turning over his business to his daughter and her husband, he realized that he could take only so much TV before he descended into the depths of despair, remembering the good TV shows of the past. Although, as a young man, he had enjoyed reading, he avoided doing so now … a tiny flying pebble propelled from his lawn mower had ricocheted off a tree, leaving him with a damaged right eye. Reading resulted in that eye tiring very quickly; the idea of audiobooks was anathema to him … "I don't 'audio' books!" He'd never had, or made, the opportunity to develop hobbies. Bill and his wife had always enjoyed a wonderful marriage relationship, but he now sensed that Ruth didn't cotton to the idea of him being underfoot all day long. In fact, one evening while his wife was on the phone with her best friend, Bill's sharp ears heard her exasperated "I do wish Bill would find something to do. There are only so many household appliances that need fixing, and he's already painted the outside of the house and put on new soffits and fascia. But he's so good at that stuff that he got it all done in the first week, and now he just sits around and, when he does get up, he's in my way." When Bill heard that, in the interests of both his wife's sanity and his own restlessness, he had decided to peruse the want ads in the community paper. There he saw that Parkview School was in need of an assistant janitor. Bill knew he had lots to offer. He could fix anything, prevent breakdowns of most equipment, and even look after boilers and air conditioning systems. He personally delivered a hand-scribbled summary of his work experience to the school office. During the subsequent interview, Bill gave his total attention to what was being asked and then responded clearly to the questions, whether they were general or specific. Both Mr. Carmichael and Horatio were impressed with Bill's wide range of knowledge … even to the specifics of products and services available to the custodial profession. His answers were succinct … in fact, almost curt … but always respectful. While Bill was obviously a good choice, he was older and … how long would he stay? He was asked that specific question. "Honestly, I don't know," he responded, then smiling, "Maybe until my wife wants me back!" Then, more seriously, "For the foreseeable future … I have no intention of looking anywhere else, but would do so if I'm not your successful candidate."

Jeff Monahan, on the other hand, giving the visual impression of being something between a motorcycle racer and a downhill mountain biker, was a 19-year-old human dynamo. Early in life he had been diagnosed as hyperactive. Little had changed since then. But his hyperactivity seemed, almost always, to have been channeled in positive directions. He was a bright student sporting a B+ average throughout high school. The reason it wasn't higher was simply because he'd participated in the marching band, the glee club, the debating club, and the varsity hockey team. No one ever saw him take a text or an assignment home. He always seemed to get his work done during school hours … other students were in awe of his ability. Even though he didn't need the extra credits, he took a basic business course ("I'm going to be a Wall Street CEO someday") as well as an optional advanced trigonometry course offered by a retired university math prof who loved the subject and called the school "my mission field". In the evenings and on weekends Jeff worked two part-time jobs, one in Gleam 'N Clean car wash, and the other at Jose's Chili 'n Fries. At Jose's establishment (Jose had long since passed away … his 50ish nephew now ran it), while yet a senior, he'd been promoted to Friday and Saturday evening manager. He was genuinely disappointed that he didn't enjoy either employment. Having graduated just before his 17th birthday, Jeff and a friend who, for some unknown reason called himself "Cipher" (he never revealed to Jeff the name his parents had given him, but Jeff figured it was Cipherius), rode their bicycles all the way from Chicago to Portland, Maine. From there they had biked back up through Vermont, and then up into Québec where they enjoyed the beautiful Eastern townships and even visited the famous "Parc Safari". Leaving the lions and the rhinos (after sampling the delicious, orchard-ripe McIntosh apples … which just happened to fall when you gave the branch only a little shake), they hiked nearby Mont St. Bruno and then they'd headed back to New York State and on through Pennsylvania and, eventually, back home. Breathlessly, Jeff offered all this unasked-for information within the first five or six minutes of meeting his interviewers. Leaning towards his interviewers, knowing they'd be spellbound with his next expostulation and, without being asked, he told them about his family … his father was on the county board, his mother was a pastry chef at Chez Papa's; his older sister, Beth, was taking political science at Elmhurst and his next older brother, "Jimbo" (James) was 6'8" and kept bumping his head on the top of the automatic garage door. He had two younger twin sisters, Joy and identical Jeanie. They were already 13 years old and he still couldn't reliably guess who was who. Their grades were identical, and their characteristics could not be distinguished one from the other. He also admitted to having a twin brother who was what he called a "no account", apparently somewhere under a tent, homeless (but never sleepless) in Seattle. Although the interviewers could easily have guessed it, Jeff, with an air of assured confidence, proclaimed, "I love to be busy, and I guarantee you I'll do a good job. You will not be disappointed with me, I assure you." He ran his words together so quickly it took an almost conscious effort to keep up with him. Without seeming to draw a desperately needed breath or giving the interviewers even a rare chance to speak, he began, rather forcefully, to relate the unasked-for information about once having met Robin Ventura (at Chez Papa's), one of the best third basemen of all time … he'd played for the White Sox for nine or ten years. Panting for a moment, catching his breath, and then, as an afterthought, he paused for a millisecond and asked, "Can I have next June and July off? Cipher and I are planning a bike trip to San Diego next year." After a short pause, upon seeing the slightest change in expression in the faces of his interviewers, he slowed down perceptibly and, with shoulders noticeably sagging, avowed, "That would be a dealbreaker for me."

Until Jeff had begun rambling, Mr. Carmichael and Horatio readily admitted to each other later, they had both initially been inclined to go with the 19-year-old dynamo. They had immediately appreciated his gung-ho enthusiasm, but they had soon tired of his incessant talking. Jeff's unrelenting chatter and ceaseless prattling would be painfully taxing. And, apparently, Jeff was of the opinion that, like teachers, it was commonplace for janitors to get a couple of months of vacation in summer. Of course, June and July were when the deep clean and waxing operations were done in the school hallways, classrooms, and the two gymnasiums. All hands needed to be on deck. Jeff's request for two months off was, indeed, a deal breaker. Jeff had just made their decision easy.

For some reason, Jeff's pace of speech slowed somewhat after they thanked them for his time. He looked almost melancholy as he headed for the exit. The last thing they saw him do was to turn around and say, "You should see the Adirondacks … they're beautiful, and in October the leaves are so ---." At that point the interview room door happened to gently close.

Both Horatio and Mr. Carmichael breathed a sigh of relief when the interview room door returned to its latched state. True, it had not slammed shut, although it had started to do so.

As in each of the other cases, Jeff had been told he would hear from them within the next few days. All four unsuccessful applicants received notes of thanks for taking the time to be interviewed and were wished well for their futures. These four found themselves having to search for other opportunities, leaving Bill Withers as the successful candidate.

An independent outsider, listening in, may have hoped that the unsuccessful candidates would have given some thought as to why they were not selected. Indeed, as they turned in for the night, each one probably did internalize their experiences. Hopefully, Harriman, upon seeing actively employed men, gave some thought to cleaning up his slothful act. Hopefully, Maggie did some soul-searching as to why people should be put off just because she tried to be neat in appearance. Hopefully, Serena may have given some consideration to the fact that it might not be in her best interest to employ her ample feminine charms as she proceeded through the job application process. And, hopefully, Jeff would think about letting prospective employers speak during interviews; he may even have to re-align some of his priorities.

The interviews were over. Now, however, other challenges awaited.

CHAPTER 10

MELODY'S CHALLENGES - EXPECTED AND UNEXPECTED

Melody had begun her work with Windy City Financial Services and quickly discovered that she enjoyed this new challenge. Of course, she had been hired by Mr. Scrivens upon the recommendation of Mrs. Golding who, in a personal visit that lasted 15 to 20 minutes more than the allotted one hour, advised her former boss, "Keep your eye on this gal – she may well surprise you with her intuitive knowledge of numbers and her pleasant way of dealing with people." Taking Patricia Golding's advice to heart, Anthony Scrivens did, indeed, carefully track the performance of his newest employee. The first responsibility she was given was to answer the phone, arrange the meeting schedule for clients ("Very important responsibility," she was told), and provide coffee for the staff, as well as for clients while they waited for their meeting with whichever accountant had been assigned to them.

Two weeks went by, and Melody had not yet made an error. The two-storey office building in which she worked was neither large nor

59

ostentatious but was located on a well-travelled street – which resulted in a fair amount of drop-in business. Almost all the 20 or so people who worked in the office made her feel most welcome. Admittedly, there was one woman, Evadne Laverock by name, who for some totally unknown reason, appeared to take an instantaneous dislike of her. But Melody looked on the bright side – the cup was more than half full. She was feeling good about herself, not only because of satisfaction with her personal performance, but also because her immediate supervisor, Betsy Watkins, confided to her that Mr. Scrivens was, as he had assured her, "suitably impressed" with Melody's efforts. That passed-along compliment put a smile on her face and boosted her ego … maybe a bit more than was healthy.

The very next day, after hearing that much appreciated compliment, Melody made what turned out to be a serious blunder. Her desk was situated in such a way that, not only could she see people as they entered from outside, from the elevator or from the second-floor stairs, but she also had a window which provided total awareness of what was going on outside. That Thursday morning, around 9:30 AM, the phone rang. Melody picked up the receiver and heard the business-like voice, "This is Verna Newman, and I'd like to make an appointment to see Mr. Scrivens. Could you put me down for Tuesday or Wednesday morning next week? I'd like an early time, say 8 o'clock or at latest, 8:30 AM." Melody checked the appointment book, and confirmed Tuesday at 8 o'clock. Ms. Newman thanked her, and they wished one another a good day.

The next Tuesday Ms. Newman showed up promptly at 8 AM. Melody rang Mr. Scrivens; the call went to voicemail. At that point, whatever it was that was creeping up her spine did not provide her with a marked degree of comfort. Why wasn't Mr. Scrivens in the office? Then, like a thunderbolt, it hit her. On Wednesday of the previous week, while Melody had been on her way to the coffee room (for what Horatio referred to as "your 10 o'clock feeding"), Betsy had met her in the hallway and told her that Mr. Scrivens would be in Philadelphia the next Tuesday. Melody had distributed coffee to the various offices, then returned to her reception desk. She had totally and irretrievably forgotten Betsy's comment about Mr. Scrivens' trip. Obviously, it hadn't been in his appointment book when Ms. Newman called.

It so happened that Ms. Newman had been courted (in the business sense) by Anthony Scrivens for almost 3 years. They had met at an accounting conference (specifically to do with the clothing industry) in Milwaukee where they had gotten to know each other casually. Scrivens, due to his keen business instincts, sensed at the time that Verna Newman wasn't exactly enamored with her business accountant. The entrepreneur and the Windy City CPA boss had been in occasional contact since that time, and it was looking more and more as if Windy City would soon have a new client. Verna was the owner and CEO of "Urban Elegance", a small chain of three stores selling women's fashions; two stores were in Illinois (Oakbrook Terrace and Decatur) and another in Lafayette, Indiana. These stores accounted for about 40% of her business … the bulk of her income came via Internet sales. She maintained a warehouse across the street from her Decatur store. Ms. Newman had visited Minneapolis on Monday where she had explored a possible new brick and mortar location; she had flown in very early on this particular Tuesday morning.

When Ms. Newman realized that her trip to Windy City was in vain – after she had arisen at 3:30 AM (after getting into bed well after midnight because of a late dinner and yet another meeting) to get to the airport by 5 AM, well, it wouldn't be a far reach to say that "the fur flew". Ms. Newman's personality was such that, on real or perceived evil intention, or oversights on someone's part, she would explode. All along the hall corridor, heads were seen peering out, looking very concerned. "What kind of a (expletive deleted) business is this? If you can't get appointments right, how can anyone expect you to do their accounting properly?"

Fortunately for everyone concerned, Ms. Newman's character wasn't all bad. She blew up quickly, but also calmed down just as quickly. While it was still quite evident that she was not pleased with the massive glitch, she attempted a smile for Melody, and even gave sort of an apology. "I've got a lunch appointment and am busy the rest of today, but I'd like to reschedule. I do want to talk to Mr. Scrivens. When did he say he'd be getting back?" After excusing herself in order to touch base with Betsy, Melody responded with, "Mr. Scrivens will be back late this afternoon, but would be available at 8:00 AM tomorrow." "Good," replied Ms. Newman, "I'll make a few adjustments in my schedule and meet with him then."

At this point, Melody, feeling lower than a snake's belly in the proverbial wagon rut, remembered a couple of sage sayings. One of them she'd learned in Sunday School: "Let him who stands take heed lest he fall." She thought that passage was somewhere in Corinthians. The other saying was of an equally warning nature, and not that different from the Bible verse: "When you stand tall, be wary of the fall." Lesson learned. Always carry a pad of paper with you.

Of course, when Scrivens did return late that afternoon, Melody herself (before anyone else could do so) knocked on Mr. Scrivens' door and, upon entry, told him the whole sad story. The "big boss" (as he was almost lovingly referred to by the accountants and staff) looked at Melody for what seemed to be a very long time but was actually only for about 15 seconds – still, it seemed an eternity. Then he spoke. "Melody, what you did or, should I say, didn't do, is very serious. That kind of oversight on your part can be very costly to a company such as ours. Think for a moment. Ms. Newman's business, if we get it, will net us somewhere in the area of $20-$22,000 each year. If she continues to give us her business for 10 years, we'd be looking at a net profit of $200,000. If I didn't know her as well as I do, this oversight on your part could have been a very costly mistake. However, from what your supervisor has told me and the vibes I've been getting from the rest of the staff, I know you have been doing an admirable job and I also know that you will learn from this mistake."

Anthony Scrivens then eased into a more contemplative mood as he, in a fatherly way, conversed with Melody. The deepening furrows in his dark face seemed, to Melody, to relax as he began to reminisce. "Melody, let me tell you something about myself. I was born and raised here in South Chicago – just another little black kid. I had two loving parents. But I hardly remember my dad. I was only four when he died. My mother and my maiden auntie raised me and my two-year-older sister. We were very poor. But my mother always told me not to bemoan my situation or feel sorry for myself, but to 'get my head on straight' and see what I could do to make something of myself. I didn't always follow her advice, I admit, and I did have some opportunities to make good money. But those opportunities always seemed to be somewhere south of the law. In fact, I will never forget my buddy, Arnold Kinkaid. He was as close to a best friend that a guy could ever have. We had so much fun together as kids. Then, when we were about 11, we were playing catch with a beat-up old pigskin on a sand lot next to the street. The cars that travelled that pot-holed street were usually beat-up old clunkers whose driveability was not enhanced by the roadway. To see anything like a late model car was rare. Then, and I remember it well, this shiny silver Range Rover SUV eased to a halt right next to us. Out of the driver's door came a handsome young man. We could see that he had a very beautiful girl with him, sitting on the passenger side and smiling kindly at us. I will make a long story short, Melody. Although the young man did not introduce himself, saying that we'd get to know him by and by, he offered us each $50 if we would take two small packages to a couple of addresses nearby. Something told me that I shouldn't do it, and I told him thanks but that I'd not do it. Well, he smiled ingratiatingly, assuring me that was okay, no problem. He then offered Arnold $100 to deliver both packages. Arnold jumped at the idea of easy money. Today Arnold is still jumping, but now he's jumping rope in the gym in the Metropolitan Correction Centre. He'd gotten deeper and deeper into the drug world until there seemed to be no way out. He evaded justice for years, decades in fact. But eventually it all caught up with him. I reached out to him a couple of times, but I don't think he wants to talk to me. He is only too aware of how a split-second decision changed two vulnerable lives. Since that fateful day where the two of us were just having fun throwing a football, I have often thought of an unalterable truism in life: 'We can choose our actions, but we can never choose their consequences.'"

Mr. Scrivens continued, "Well, Melody, to this day I thank God and the guidance of my mother … it served me well for the decision I made when I was 11 years old. As I look back on it now, I believe that was the best decision, or at least one of the most significant, that I've made in my lifetime. I even started to pay more attention to my teachers and as I progressed through junior high and entered high school, I found that I really enjoyed numbers. I did really well at math but, don't tell anyone, my marks in the language arts were abysmal. I loved numbers – to this day I remember my grade 8 math teacher, his jaw hanging open and with an unbelieving look on his face as I mentally added up column after column of three-digit numbers in 10 seconds and sometimes less. All of which is to say, I l-o-v-e-d numbers. Getting into the accounting world was just a natural progression for me. I started doing minor tasks for a small accounting firm and soon realized I could do a lot better if I started my own business. That, in itself, is another story that I won't get into detail now. Suffice to say, I began in the basement of my mother's home, but that didn't last very long. Sixteen months later I had three "clients" … just small business folks who wanted me to collate their invoices and receipts, and then add up columns for them … one of whom was actually the owner of a moderately-sized business and, maybe more significantly, a good friend of my deceased father. Of course, he had to take my accounting work to a real CPA. Apparently, the auditor who eventually saw the work I'd done (I'd made a bunch of notes and suggestions) was impressed. And, because of that auditor (and, eventually, my own certification as a CPA), much more business was sent my way. And, Melody, the rest is history. I guess, in all this, what I'm trying to tell you is that we need to pay close attention to everything we do, and we need to make good decisions in life, whether those decisions are financial, moral, physical, or spiritual. And, Melody, I want to encourage you to stick with what you know are good decisions, even when they are the difficult or less desirable alternative."

"Melody, I want to thank you for taking the time to listen to me. Please do not beat yourself up over the mistake you made. I respect you for immediately coming in to see me as soon as you could. You are a fine young woman with some seriously good potential. In fact, I'd like for you to consider a career in accounting. Although you have been doing a fine job as receptionist – and all that it entails (but anybody can deliver coffee) – I'm going to hire another person for that job. No", and he chuckled, "I'm not firing you! What I want you to do now, starting early next week, is to spend a week with each of our accountants, just shadowing what they do. Listen to their conversations with clients. Learn from each of the accountants and try to grasp what their strengths and weaknesses are. Of course, I don't want you instructing them … that's not your role … nor do I want you to say anything more than "Hi" to our clients! But I do want you to learn from each and every one of my CPAs. I have good people in those roles. You may find Mr. Ravenshadow somewhat cold at first – he's still a little old-fashioned when it comes to females in business – but with your pleasant personality, he may soon warm to you. He is very good at what he does, and you will learn a lot from him. Who knows? He may be your strongest supporter as you go on for your CPA!"

With that, Mr. Scrivens stood up and told her to enjoy the rest of her day.

Melody couldn't wait to share that day's experiences with Horatio. Somehow, the classic movie "The Good, The Bad, and The Ugly" kept coming to mind. There was more of each to come.

CHAPTER 11

EMBRACING TRIUMPHS – CONFRONTING CHALLENGES

That evening, sitting down at the two-person card table in the basement of their (temporary) newlywed home, enjoying fried eggs, pork and beans, and a lettuce salad that her mother had brought down to them, Melody told Horatio the whole story. She left out nothing. As Horatio dug into his repast which was served on old Melmac dishes they'd picked up at a garage sale, he took turns furrowing his brow and, at appropriate times, smiling as the story was shared with him. True to form, Melody shared many words, describing all the nuances of her conversation with Mr. Scrivens, finally – some 10 minutes later – concluding with the exciting news of her changed job description. She was going to be paid to learn! When she told Horatio that Mr. Scrivens had even hinted that there might be a little surprise in her next paycheck, they simultaneously got up, hugged, and did the dance of joy. If all of life was going to be this enjoyable, wow, wasn't this going to be fun!!

That night, as they snuggled into their bed next to the furnace room with the on-again off-again cacophony of the air conditioner, a happier couple could not have been found. Not in Chicago, not even in all of Illinois. They talked about Melody's experience for a goodly while, reminding one another that little oversights and mistakes can lead to major repercussions. Anything that they may have done later is none of our business.

As far as they were concerned, their little hovel was a castle, and they were the king and queen. They were going to keep their pledge to each other not to produce any little princes or princesses for at least three or four years. They needed to get established. Over a breakfast of oatmeal and toast the next morning, they reinforced their decision. Their two-burner hotplate didn't allow for much variety in their diet at any particular meal. When Emily unexpectedly gifted them with a toaster oven, their joy was complete! Well, almost.

Life became busy for both of them. Melody loved the new responsibility of learning from the CPAs at Windy City. Of course, she was not only learning, but also assisting with searching out files and finding appropriate resources so that the accountants could do their jobs more efficiently. Sometimes, she was even asked to get some coffee for the client; this usually happened only when Willow Bertsch, the new receptionist, was busy on the phone. Melody didn't mind doing these little favours once in a while, and she didn't complain. However, to herself she admitted that she would have preferred sitting in on the entire discussion between CPA and client.

Week after week went by, and she was learning much about the world of accounting. She realized how meticulous the CPAs were. They had to do everything according to government regulation, but they used those regulations to prepare tax forms that included as many tax deductions as possible. They prided themselves in proving their ads to be true: "We Work for YOU". As a result, they had many happy clients. And, as for the IRS, they rarely found errors so they, too, were happy. Well, given the bureaucratic propensity to collect as much as possible, "happy" may not be strictly accurate. But Windy City Financial Services never gave the IRS reason for suspicion.

It was with some trepidation when it came Melody's turn to spend a week in Mr. Ravenshadow's office. Of course, she had seen him many times, but he never really established eye contact with her, nor did he ever greet her, implying that he wasn't even aware of her existence. At least, that's what she thought. This was going to be a contrast to the pleasantries she'd experienced with Higgins, Bartelli, Washington, and Davis.

Cedric Ravenshadow differed from the other CPAs in a multitude of ways. To young Melody, he was both formidable and intimidating. In appearance, his facial features were gnarled and craggy, giving him a truly fearsome, almost cadaverous, presence. Wherever he went, it always seemed to the onlooker that he was following his nose, whichever direction it desired to proceed. Not only did he have an unusually large proboscis, but it had been subject to a considerable pounding in his youth when he'd experienced inordinately many unexpected uppercuts in the boxing ring. When Melody first saw him 'not looking' at her in the hallway, she immediately thought of Scrooge. His weathered visage gave the impression of one who has spent 50 winters in Antarctica and hadn't enjoyed one moment of it. Though, as senior CPA, he had the luxury of a corner office, even that did not seem to put a smile on his face. For all his adult life, Ravenshadow had been a pipe smoker. His normally morose nature became even more pronounced the year that Anthony Scrivens proclaimed Windy City Financial Services a no-smoking zone. Cedric had offered significant rebellion at what he called "this outrageous law". He even pursued other CPA employment opportunities, asking them at the beginning of the interview whether or not they allowed smoking. Every one of them had introduced the same ridiculous ruling. So he was stuck with Windy City. Having always enjoyed smoking pipes (and at home he still did), he had an amazing collection of pipes, ranging from a genuine antique corncob pipe from Tennessee to a mahogany pipe engraved with his initials. The latter he'd purchased "on sale" for the price of $1395. Every time he held that pipe (he smoked it only once), an observer would have seen a slight contemplative smile interrupt his reverie.

Cedric Ravenshadow had been in the accounting business his entire life. Well, almost. His father had been an accountant "in some small hick town" as he, later that week, described his early life to Melody. But communications with Melody on that first Monday morning were not overly cordial. His first word to her, if it could have been described as a word, was "Harrumph". Although that word had not yet appeared in any extant dictionary of the English language, the intent of it was clear to Melody. This wasn't going to be easy.

As if the challenge of listening and watching the interaction between CPA and client wasn't enough of a challenge, it soon became apparent that this was not going to be a good day. The first client to see "the Raven" (as the mail boy had nicknamed him) was a lady of about 38 or 40 who had a home business ("Creationary") of producing unique party favors and decorative knickknacks. Olivia Brightwell was a fun-loving lady who looked 25 and, because of her seeing humor everywhere, sometimes acted as if she was 9 or 10. She was given to giggling at the slightest provocation. Not even a minute after Cedric's "harrumph" greeting in his office, in walked Olivia. She had sparkling green eyes and a smile on her face that was obviously permanent, if the easily detectable laugh lines around her mouth were any indication of reliability.

The meeting began sanely enough. Ravenshadow greeted Olivia with a quick "Hello, let's get right down to business." Olivia had been told that Melody would be there to watch and learn. With those first abrupt words of what passed for Ravenshadow's greeting, Melody's and Olivia's eyes met. And, on meeting, they simultaneously recognized in each other a kindred spirit. While they quickly greeted each other, Cedric was on the phone to the receptionist Willow for coffee, but didn't get through to her, as she was obviously busy doing something else. So it was Melody who went for the coffee.

Upon her return with 3 cups of coffee, she carefully lowered the tray and set it down on the corner of the desk. However, strange things can happen. Life is that way. On setting the coffee tray on the desk, she had accidentally placed one corner of the tray on the raised stem of Ravenshadow's Meerschaum pipe which he had prominently displayed. At that point a sequence of events occurred which could only be described as seriously disconcerting. Over went all 3 cups of scalding hot coffee. The desk was huge, most suitable for a man of Cedric's vintage and experience. While the desk was large and had a vast surface area, the equivalent of at least two full cups of black liquid lava flowed swiftly toward the venerable man's location. Upon reaching the edge of the desk, the steaming liquid succumbed to gravity. Since the entire procedure took less than one full second – much less time than would have been required for an elderly man to move out of the way, the cascading coffee (1 cup of which was Olivia's decaf) descended directly on Ravenshadow's lap. It would not be an exaggeration to say that everyone on the floor heard the immediate reaction. Well, not everyone. Higgins's office was at the far end, and he'd forgotten his hearing aids that day, so he may well not have heard the painful outcry.

It was too late, of course, but Cedric leapt out of the chair with a rapidity that his body had not experienced for, at least, the past three decades. Upon watching him leap about grimacing with the inevitable initial pain associated with hot liquids on tender skin, Olivia happened to glance at Melody. As their eyes met, for reasons that have never yet been fully analyzed by any human behavior PhD candidate, the two females broke into hysterical giggling at what had happened to the unfortunate septuagenarian. Cedric glared at them, initially uttering unprintable words, but gradually calming down and muttering under his breath. The ladies distinctly heard him say, "Women! What are they doing in a man's business world?" Upon hearing this, the 'girls' were bent over with tears, helpless with laughter. Although separated in years by well over a decade, they were both 9 again.

As Cedric Ravenshadow's unexpected agony began to subside, he was finally able to observe his surroundings. Initially he looked at his wet pants, then at the liquid on his desk and office chair and then, as if a new sight was revealing itself to him, he saw the women. Both were literally gasping for breath between laughs. When Olivia half slipped off her chair, falling onto one knee, with renewed vigor more peals of laughter ensued. At that point, even Cedric couldn't help but crack a long dormant smile. As the ladies gradually were able to begin the monumental task of controlling themselves, he saw the tear-tracked faces where their mascara had apparently decided to undertake a voyage to their respective jaws. With an ever-broadening smile on his own face, he gingerly walked over to the console table under the side window where he picked up a box of Kleenex that had been placed there some years earlier. He opened it and brought it to the women. By this time, everything was funny. A new round of nearly uncontrollable laughter made its appearance. By this time, even Ravenshadow was chuckling noticeably.

Finally, order was restored, at least to some degree. The actual business began about 10 minutes later, following cleanup of the desk and chair, a change of apparel for Cedric, and the fixing of faces by the ladies. Although there were momentary lapses into short giggles with even "the Raven" breaking into a short chortle on occasion, they were finally able to get the necessary work done.

That episode was the best thing that could have happened. The ice was broken between Melody and her "boss of the week". From that point on Cedric Ravenshadow, the moody bachelor, developed what seemed to be a new appreciation for the fair sex, and he was prepared, at least partially, to allow them into his business world. By Wednesday, Cedric was already in teaching mode, asking Melody questions like "Do you know why I asked Mrs. Higginbotham about her not reporting the tips she got while driving her cab? And what about Mr. Gonzalez when I asked if he made any purchases for his meat shop last year?" He stressed how important it was to watch people's faces and their body language to determine whether or not they were reporting all their income and, just as important, whether they were reporting all their expenses.

Meanwhile, Horatio was also experiencing life's challenges, not all of which were, in retrospect, as enjoyable as Melody's.

CHAPTER 12

FLAMES, BLAMES, AND CLAIMS

Back in the days when Horatio was volunteering to stack chairs and help out wherever he could in the school, he, of course, had no idea that he would one day be a janitor. He could not even have imagined being the head janitor. For all he knew at the time, the janitor was responsible for keeping the school clean. That was it.

When he'd been officially hired as janitor, he began to realize that there was a lot more to this job than appeared on the surface. Not only was there a myriad of products used for cleaning various surfaces, but he had to learn details concerning things like times between applications, how strong to mix the solutions and, more recently, the minutia of ordering materials well before he ran out of a particular product. He had to report to, and attend, the Workplace Safety and Health quarterly committee meetings. In addition, there were the state-mandated health and safety presentations. Then there was the need to learn to prioritize duties, no easy task while, at the same time, dealing with many that presented themselves without any advance warning. Somewhere, he'd heard of "mind maps" and he even considered the possibility of using one, but didn't do so, figuring that would be just another consumer of his already limited time availability. On occasion, though, he wondered about that decision. The need to keep in good shape, he believed, was part and parcel of the job, as there was often heavy lifting involved. Then there were the more elusive responsibilities that required more focus mentally than physically. Horatio had to understand the basics of the machinery necessary in any modern school – heating and cooling systems, kitchen appliances in the cafeteria, etc. – this area was not a great concern because much of it seemed to come naturally to him. He knew all about built-in obsolescence and the associated need to be aware of various things that could go wrong, and how soon that might happen. This was an area where Horatio's value was really appreciated by the school administrators. It wasn't something that was readily visible, but in his biweekly reports to Principal Radner as to his activities, his boss was quite aware of the money that Horatio was saving for the school. Mr. Radner even made it a point to mention Horatio's good work to the school superintendent. Horatio's efficiency was even reported to the Board and was mentioned in the Board's newsletter to the school community.

Another significant area in which his mental faculties had to be attuned was to relate kindly, not only to fellow workers and teachers, but especially to the students. Because of his caring nature and acceptance by most of the students, he didn't see this as a significant problem or challenge. He often reported back to Melody, "I just love the kids. The young people seem to really appreciate me." When meeting them, he got a smile from almost everyone.

There was one situation, however, that began to bother him a bit. One of the grade 10 girls, Cherry Treadley, but nicknamed "Cheerio" because she was almost always morose, began, after a few weeks into the new term, to smile at him. "Oh," he confidently assured himself, "she's finally coming out of her negative attitude to life." He had wondered what kind of existence she had outside of school and felt a bit sorry for her. So, when she smiled at him, he returned a genuine smile of his own. Soon, however, he sensed that she was often within his vicinity. If he had a call from a certain classroom teacher, asking him to check a window sash with a noticeable crack around the edge, for some reason, the hairs on the back of his neck would begin to rise. He'd look around and there, not very far off, was Cherry.

When she caught his eye looking at her she smiled, but turned away, pretending that she was on her way to another destination. At first, Horatio didn't think much of these episodes, but when they began to happen repeatedly, Horatio sensed that there might be a wily fox hiding behind the woodpile. He even went so far as to mention it to Mr. Radner, just so that, if anything untoward happened, he wanted the principal to be aware of the situation. Then, Thursday afternoon just after the lunch hour, he had a fairly large cleanup job to look after in the cafeteria. Someone had accidentally spilled a jug of milk on the floor, in a corner of the room near the easily accessible refrigerator. By the time he got to the scene (he had been briefly out of the school getting a power bar for one of the teachers), most of the students had gone back to class and Horatio, mop in one hand and a pail of water in the other (it brought back memories of the day after his engagement) he whistled softly as he proceeded to the worksite. On arriving he began cleaning up. Soon he was down on his knees, wiping the baseboards and even the walls where the milk had splashed. He heard footsteps softly approaching from behind and, looking back, he saw Cheerio. "Oh, hi, Cherry," he smiled, "lunch hour is over – you are late." His comment elicited a sultry "Hi there," and a smile that, all men recognize, is more than a mere smile of friendship. That smile brought back vague memories of Serena Blake.

Not only had Horatio taken various courses directly associated with his janitorial responsibilities, but Principal Radner had also insisted that all staff and teachers take that "Dealing with Amorous Teenagers" three-hour course that was offered once a year. His certification in this course proved to be very useful at this point. His recollections of what to do in this situation kicked in immediately. "Don't you have biology in 3A right now?" "Yes," she replied huskily, "But right now I have a biology class in the cafeteria." With that obvious intent on her part, Horatio's response was swift. "Cherry, please come to the principal's office with me. Tell Mr. Radner what you just not-so-subtly proposed to me." The suggestive look in her eyes quickly turned into anger. "I'll tell Mr. Radner that you tried to force yourself on me," she railed. "Okay, Cherry, come with me to the principal's office and tell him that, too. But, be aware that I have already informed him what I figured you might be thinking about doing, and let's see how he reacts." With that offer, Cherry let out a hurt, but angry scream. As Cherry ran out of the cafeteria, Horatio heard her crying. Part of him felt sorry for her, but he went directly to the principal's office, and informed Mr. Radner of exactly what had happened. The principal put an understanding hand on Horatio's shoulder and assured him, "I'm not surprised, Horatio. Brom Beeker, over in chemistry, has voiced the same concerns about Cherry."

Once again, Horatio had probably saved the school and himself, not only a lot of money, but also a lot of embarrassment and headache. Not to say anything about the needless potential hassle of court proceedings.

If that had been the end of the problem, it would simply have been chalked up to experience. Horatio recognized the value of the commonsense approach that he had used, and it reinforced within him the necessity of responding similarly if another such situation should arise. That evening Melody praised him for his wise course of action. Whew, that was over. Horatio's sleep was uninterrupted by dreams. He knew he had done the right thing.

That is, his sleep was uninterrupted until 2:15 AM. At that unearthly hour he heard sirens wailing a few streets over. Getting out of bed, climbing the stairs, and looking out of the window, he saw a thin trail of smoke rising in the moonlit night. He hoped it wasn't someone's house and prayed that no one was injured. As he descended the stairs, hoping he could get back to sleep, he heard the phone ring. By the time he'd re-climbed the stairs and got to the phone, it had rung five times and, by then, his in-laws were up as well. His mother-in-law offered, "I'll get that. I know my aunt in Little Rock is ill, and she may be calling me." Upon answering and, with both a momentary sense of relief and then renewed concern, she gave the phone to Horatio. "I think it's Mr. Radner, and he sounds pretty agitated." Without any unnecessary words, the principal informed Horatio that there was a fire at the school, and could he get there quickly? "I'll be there as fast as I can," responded Horatio, and added, "Should I get Bill Withers to come?" "No, responded the principal … he's the one who called me … the emergency vehicles drove right by his house."

Horatio's trusty Chevrolet got him to the school in record time, although the potholed pavement didn't do the car's suspension any good. There were two police cruisers on the scene but only one fire truck. Mr. Radner was already there, talking with one of the firemen. As Horatio approached to where the two men were talking, the Fire Chief emerged from the school's main entrance, strode down the short walkway to the street where the police were making sure that no unauthorized personnel would enter the school. Fire Chief Diego Valdez, built like a professional wrestler, to everyone's immense relief, announced "The fire's out. We were able to suppress it with foam. But there will be quite a cleanup job necessary in the girl's washroom as well as in much of the east end of the school."

Valdez' next, somber comment, was totally unexpected. In what was his trademark laconic style, he stated, "We believe it was arson. That's another reason for the police presence. They're bringing in an arson specialist and even a tracking dog. We found about 10 or 12 wet sheets of Kleenex stuffed into one of the garbage receptacles. Someone was doing a lot of crying. The kicker that convinced us that it was arson was a message on the bathroom mirror written in red lipstick. It simply read, 'I hate HJ'." Horatio stood there, stunned. The earlier events of the day were described to the police, Horatio himself supplying most of the information. Principal Radner corroborated Horatio's story.

Using the Kleenex as scent bait, the tracking dog soon located Cherry. She had somehow found her way into the presumably locked teachers' lounge where she was lying on a couch, sobbing pitifully. When Officer Susan Workman questioned her as to her motive for starting a fire, between sobs she blubbered, "I just want to die. Nobody loves me."

When Cherry voiced that heartbroken comment, even the toughened 6'5" Diego Valdez found it necessary to ask patrol officer Workman for Kleenex. With a break in his voice, he simply observed, "Some kids have it so hard." Officer Workman ensured that she kept a few of the absorbent wipes for herself as she felt a certain sensation of moisture in the corner of her eyes. Valdez himself had five children, three of them teen girls. He promised himself that he would spend much more time with his children. That second golf game of the week would be deleted from his schedule.

Needless to say, there was discussion as to whether or not Cherry should be charged for her crime. While Sgt. Brock Bigelow (a mere 6'2"), the driver of the second squad car, was scribbling details for that purpose in his notepad, Horatio was whispering to Mr. Radner. The principal stepped closer to the Sergeant and, almost conspiratorially, said, "Horatio has an idea that I think all of us need to seriously consider. Cherry is obviously hurting, not only from today's events, but probably also from other things that are going on in her life. Would you, as law enforcement officers, be willing to let us deal with Cherry? Horatio has offered to consult with his wife and myself to provide Cherry with an opportunity for some genuine friendship, letting her know that she is of as much value as anyone else. If Melody – that's Horatio's wife – is willing, I think we can help rectify Cherry's situation without putting her through even more trauma." Sgt. Bigelow, after a brief consultation with Officer Workman, agreed to the unusual suggestion and tore up his notes. Bigelow presented just one caveat: "We're going to check with you every week or two for the first couple months. We don't need any more firebugs roaming the streets. But we realize this is kind of a special case and, who knows, it may provide a good case study for further consideration by our department."

There was significant fallout from this entire experience, not only for Horatio, Emily, Cherry, and Principal Radner, but also for many in the community who heard what had happened. Of course, Horatio told

Melody the story and conveyed to her the misery experienced by the young girl. Melody responded, as he expected, from her caring heart. "Yes, let's help her!"

The more mundane fallout of that eventful day or, more accurately, eventful night, was the major cleanup job in the washroom as well as obliterating some serious smoke damage in the eastern wing of the school. The washroom with the actual fire damage was located at the furthest east end of the school where the roof sloped down to just 10 feet from the floor level. The fire had been started, using a pile of paper towels next to the wood paneling in one of the stalls. Across the top of the wall, 12-inch windows allowed natural lighting during the morning hours. One of the windows had been opened and was the conduit for the trail of smoke that had been visible in the area. Horatio and Bill were, of course, involved in the process of restoring the washroom and the hallways to their original condition. Many calls to work crews and insurance personnel had to be made and a great deal of manual labor done. Along with the principal and teachers, Horatio had to assist in decisions for relocation of teaching areas while the eastern part of the school was being refurbished. It was necessary to relocate three morning and afternoon classes in one gym and two classes in another. Regular gym classes had to be juggled into other time slots. Horatio had researched which restoration firm had the highest ratings while still keeping the cost reasonable. "Cinder Clear Restoration" was his recommendation. Their quote was mid-range. His suggestion was forwarded on to the board. The school's board did their own research and found that Horatio's suggestion was a wise one. Cinder Clear was able to send out a crew within a week (timing was another significant issue). Horatio was able to provide good ideas to the crew (one of which was a new-on-the-market product called "FreshFireFix" which even the restoration people hadn't heard of, but immediately began using), and they welcomed him to their coffee breaks. He made use of more than a couple of those opportunities. Most of the time, however, he had too many other priorities which needed attention. It took the restoration crew two days fewer than the three weeks they had quoted. The quote, at Horatio's recommendation, was prepared on a 'per 8-hour day' basis. The two fewer days meant a savings of over $1250 in labor costs to the board. Naturally, the insurer was pleased with the smaller bill as well. After the workmen left for the day, Horatio usually enlisted the help of Bill Withers to help with the cleanup of the work area. Horatio was a busy janitor … and he had a willing helper. Bill's wife no longer had reason to complain to her best friend. Bill was underfoot no longer.

As for Cherry's situation, although hesitant at first, she realized that she was being given something very special by people who really seemed to care for her. While in Melody's company, it appeared to Cherry that whoever Melody knew loved her. Cherry herself turned out to be no exception. By the third visit with Melody, Cherry viewed Melody as a big sister. They cried together and they laughed together. As suspected, Cherry's home situation had not been positive, and even now was not good. Her father had left the family 14 months ago and Cherry's mother, Rebecca, was on welfare. Having no marketable skills, her mother, a high school dropout, did a lot more searching for work than finding work. Sometimes she became seriously despondent and had even taken to drinking more than most people would consider 'enough'. Cherry and her little brother often came to school hungry. Melody was able to relate to Cherry how Horatio had grown up in somewhat similar financial circumstances, but had applied himself diligently and, as Cherry knew only too well, was now head janitor at the school.

Then, at prescribed times, Cherry and Melody met with Horatio and Principal Radner to review how things were going. Sgt. Bigelow attended only the first of those meetings and 10 minutes of the second, confiding to Mr. Radner, "There is no point in my being here, I'm just in the way. Cherry is doing so well with you guys. In fact, I'm going to put in a recommendation to my chief that we consider this kind of approach with juvenile offenders much more often." At the next regular meeting between the foursome, Officer Workman attended, just because she wanted to see for herself the results which Bigelow had related to her. Once again, her tear ducts became active as she left the room.

PLANS, SURPRISES, AND FINANCES

Horatio's commitment to his father-in-law that he and his new wife would be out of the Lacoste's basement six months after their marriage, was beginning to weigh heavily on his mind. While he knew that they would willingly be allowed a grace period, he and Melody both scanned the want ads section of the local community paper as well as the ads in the real estate pamphlets that regularly appeared in their mailbox. Normally, real estate flyers were considered junk mail, but now they were perused almost religiously. It reminded them of the days when they were cramming for their senior exams.

Of course, Melody had also graduated from high school, but with much less fanfare than that which had accompanied Horatio's celebration. Melody had to be content with an online graduation ceremony because of a widespread outbreak of a virus that had struck the entire community. Of course, their families had made a big deal of

Melody's matriculation, but the health authorities had forbidden larger groups from getting together.

As they both looked at the sometimes-enhanced pictures of apartments that were available, they had to consider a number of distinct realities. Their combined annual salaries, minus all foreseen deductions, allowed them a net take-home pay of about $54,000. It was much more than enough to, at least, rent a small clean apartment. Because of what was hoped to be only a brief downturn in the economy, Mr. Scrivens had to lay Melody off during the summer months. However, he came through with his promise to pay for her online certification courses if she would commit to study during that time. Meanwhile, for the same reason, and because the district school janitors were not unionized, the expected average of 3% annual raises had not come through during the first year of their marriage. While they still set aside the monthly amount they had committed in order to buy a house within 16 years (which, until now, had been an amazing $1850 per month), they realized the going might not be quite as smooth in future as they had envisioned. Nor did they cut down on their charitable giving; they had agreed on donating $150 per month to the local food bank, $250 to the church, and the remaining $50 per month to miscellaneous charities. The total accounted for the 10% that Pastor Wilfred had suggested.

They checked in with the loans officer at the bank where Horatio had received the loan for his car. Together, the three of them reviewed the financial details. After less than a half hour of consultation, loans officer Lamar Brooks, in his immaculately pressed dress pants and bow-tied silk shirt, gave them a clean financial bill of health. "You guys are doing things right," were his welcomed words. "But continue to monitor your budget closely. As you look at the next year, remember that state taxes will see a significant jump – we still don't know exactly how much – and, not only that, but the city has already announced a 2% hike in water and sewer rates. Nor do we know yet what property taxes will be. Even if you rent an apartment, the landlords will, inevitably, be requiring a higher monthly payment."

The mixed bag of positive and negative information gleaned from Lamar Brooks reinforced the conviction of the young couple to redouble their efforts in maintaining their ultimate goals as well as to immediately "bear down" in their search for an affordable apartment. If they were going to own their own house by the 16th year of their marriage, as well as preparing for an increase in their family within four years, they agreed that they could not spend more than $800 a month on an apartment. That expense would immediately reduce their "set aside" funds to $1050 per month. While their combined income at present was quite substantial, Melody wasn't so sure that she wanted to become a full-time employee of Windy City, thinking she would sooner become a full-time mother if and when a child, or children, arrived on the scene. As much as she enjoyed going to work – and she was now working full time as Cedric Ravenshadow's assistant (it was a shocker when he asked her!) – her motherly instinct, she admitted to Horatio, was beginning to make itself known. But they both realized that, if Melody did not go to work, that would represent a very substantial drop in their income, making it more of a challenge to save, not only for a house, but also for their eventual retirement. Sooner, rather than later, they would have to do some even more serious financial planning.

The search for an apartment continued. Evening after evening, rather than watching the television (which, on occasion, worked), they scanned advertisements. Of course, there were apartments available for as low as $450 a month not far from the school or the accounting office, but they were located in a recognized danger zone of abject poverty and human degradation. Crack houses and brothels were the main features. Lots of bright lights in a dark place. A well-known renegade motorcycle gang had their "office" there. Although Melody and Horatio knew that Pastor Williams spent at least one afternoon a week in that neighborhood, inviting individuals to join him at the coffee shop where he shared his faith and hope (a former 'enforcer' and his 'bikie woman' were now members of the church), neither Melody or Horatio felt that 'hood' would be an appropriate area for them, and certainly not for any children they may have.

Yes, the search continued. There were plenty of apparently quite acceptable apartment blocks in the more northerly part of their community, but they couldn't find anything in their price range. The least expensive one in that more desirable area was $1200 a month and the price was described as "firm". There was obviously no negotiation possible there, and certainly no chance of getting the price reduced to $800. Then, one evening while they were perusing yet more advertisements, the phone rang. Melody's parents were not home – there was some 'all-employees and significant others' get-together at Frankie's workplace – so up went Horatio, almost dragging his feet. "It'll probably be another one of those scam calls," surmised Melody. Both of them had had a long day, and they, almost by mutual consent, didn't answer the phone. But they thought better of it.

Answering the phone on the fifth or sixth ring, Horatio responded cheerily, despite his weariness. The voice at the other end, sounding vaguely familiar, introduced himself with "Hi, this is Darius Thompson. You probably don't remember me, and there's no reason you should cuz it's at least two or three years ago when we first met. I was the one you spoke with at that warehouse where you came to look for a job. I went to school with your mother, and we met yesterday in a grocery aisle at Walmart. We shared some old memories of our teachers, and then she told me about you. Things clicked in my mind, and I remembered you had the same surname as Emily. "Is Horatio, by any chance, your son?" I asked her. "The long and short of it is, I understand you are looking for an apartment. I left that warehouse job and am now managing Bluebird Apartments four streets over from where your mother lives. There is an apartment available, and the people who are moving out, in just under a month, have kept the place immaculately clean. I hate to lose them, but I'd love for you to have the apartment. There's just one bathroom, but there is a nice master bedroom with a small balcony that overlooks the little creek where your mother mentioned you used to like to go fishing with your buddies. There is also a small alcove that the landlord likes to call a bedroom. It could be used as a small office. The kitchen was updated about three years ago. All the appliances, except for the range, were installed new at the time. Would you be interested?"

"Of course, we'd be interested!" was Horatio's immediate and enthusiastic response. "But," and then his voice wavered a bit, "What is the monthly rent?" Darius quickly responded, "It's only $920 a month. I'll let you in on a little secret. After the information that Emily shared with me, I informed landlord Odell Wigglesworth (I know, I also laughed when I first heard his name!) that both you and your wife have good jobs and are not only financially reliable, but also very honest people. Most of the folks in this apartment block are paying between $1020 a month and $1300 a month, depending on the size of the apartment. But, when Odell learned more about you from my description, he agreed to lower the price to $920. Now, are you still interested?"

Horatio's initial impulse was to shout, "YES, we ARE interested!" But, then, he remembered their budget and the plans that he and Melody had scrupulously put together. Those plans did not include paying $920 per month for an apartment. Horatio responded, "I've been by Bluebird Apartments many times – and not always for fishing – and I have always admired how the grounds are kept so attractive in an area that many people call 'run down'. I'm sure we would love to live there but, frankly, even $920 a month is more than our budget allows. You see, we're taking a long-term approach in our savings plan. Even though we could easily pay that amount right now, the fact is that Melody is feeling more and more convinced that she will want to be a stay-at-home mom. Not only are we saving for a house, which we hope to substantially pay for in another 15 years or so, but we are also putting aside a significant portion of our salaries into an IRA plan recommended by our loans officer at the bank. Also, Melody's boss, Mr. Scrivens, strongly endorsed the organization, Great Lakes Financial Stewards, that our loans officer had suggested we contact. In fact, Mr. Scrivens called GLFS and spoke directly to the chief 'steward' (their advisors are all called stewards), Isabella Chavez. She spoke briefly with Melody and suggested we meet her soon. From that point, she convincingly stated, we'd meet at least once a year to track any investments we make. We're really excited about our future – we love children, and we hope to have at least two or three." For just a long moment Horatio paused, suddenly remembering Jeff Monahan, the job applicant who had offered far more than the necessary information. He comforted himself with the thought that the extra information he had spouted out was, at least, obliquely related to the subject. He could almost hear Darius smiling at the other end of the phone line.

There was a pregnant silence on the line for about 12 seconds. Horatio wondered if Darius had muted the phone to cover up his chuckling at a young man's enthusiasm. But Darius finally, and seriously, responded with, "Man, I wish all of our residents would demonstrate your financial acumen. You guys are amazing! We've got some really fine people living in our apartments – we do our best to screen the applicants – but most of them sort of live hand to mouth, often buying things they don't need, and giving little thought to any goals even two years ahead, never mind 15 or 40!" There was another long pause. Then, "Let me see what I can do, if anything." With that somewhat ambiguous statement, Darius wished Horatio a good night, saying he'd get back to him in a day or two.

Horatio bounded down the steps, two at a time, almost tripping four steps from the bottom and having to grab the handrail to avoid falling on his face. "What was that all about?" he heard his bride ask as he blew open the makeshift bedroom door he had installed to provide a modicum of privacy. Horatio caught his breath and, with more enthusiasm than he normally exhibited, he fairly bubbled over as he shared Darius' news with the sweet woman obviously anticipating what he had to say.

Melody's response was less enthusiastic than Horatio had expected it would be. "That sounds wonderful, my love, but don't forget, that's just the rent. Did you ask about the utilities? What about electricity, water and sewer? Different apartments may have different regulations. I assume the taxes are paid by the owners of the apartment, but what about furniture? We don't need a lot of stuff here in this little basement, but in a two-bedroom apartment with a living room, well, dear, we both love wide open spaces, but that love doesn't really apply to a 950 ft.² apartment." Horatio responded more abruptly than he had intended, "Melody, look at the facts. We've got to get out of here soon. And we can obviously afford it!" At that point, for some reason, Horatio remembered a snippet of wisdom that Pastor Wilfred had shared with them. He had warned them about one of them wanting something very badly, and the other one putting the brakes on. The pastor had gone on to say that they were going to have to be prepared to discuss the options rationally, without raising their voices. Regretting his abrupt response, he apologized. He had seen the sudden hurt in Melody's eyes and felt the pang in his heart. Of course, Melody immediately forgave him. They agreed to wait for the promised phone call.

True to his word, Darius called as soon as he could. This time Annabelle answered the phone and called them upstairs. There was something in Annabelle's voice that, for some reason, bothered Melody. She knew her mother had been to the doctor that afternoon, but dismissed her concern because she thought her mother might just be tired. Also, she was excited about what Darius would have to say to them.

"Put your phone on speaker," Darius requested. I want both of you to hear this. "I have, what I hope will be good news for you guys. My boss, Odell Wigglesworth, has instructed me to tell you that his bottom-line offer is $850 a month, inclusive of all costs. And, my young friends, I know exactly what his cost per month is, including taxes and everything that goes with it. He is getting very close to, at best, a breakeven point. After some persuasion on my part, he agreed to give you three days to think about it before it would go on the market for its true value." Nearly in unison, but in more subdued tones than they had evidenced earlier, they voiced their thank-yous and promised to get back to Darius within the allotted three days.

That night, try as they might, they did not get much sleep. Melody even heard Horatio get out of bed at least twice, pace the basement, and even go up the stairs to the kitchen where she heard him open and close the fridge door a couple of times before descending once again to the basement. There he did a little more pacing before crawling into bed, yawning deeply, rolling over once or twice, and then finally breathing deeply. She knew her husband was finally asleep, but that didn't help her situation any. When it was time for both of them to rise, she knew that she had amassed, at most, an hour and a half of true sleep.

After proceeding through their morning rituals, they drove off to their respective workplaces, Melody dropping Horatio off at the school before she proceeded on to the accounting office. Although neither shirked their work responsibilities that day, anyone who met them quickly realized their minds were far away while they went through their typical workday activities. Despite her divided mind, Melody did not repeat any of the mistakes she had made earlier in her short career. That evening, while waiting for the call that never came, they reviewed their financial situation. In examining their savings at the bank, the 3% interest was accumulating according to schedule. Not much, but no surprises there. Then they dug into the file containing their investment statements. There they found a surprise, and it was a pleasant one. The share price of one of their two holdings (Lamar Brooks had talked them into these) had gone up 10% over the past three months. The company had rewarded their investors with a higher return on their shares. Instead of the expected 5.8%, their dividend was now at 7.5% on an annual basis. They rejoiced in the fact that they were further ahead than they had thought they'd be. They were on course financially and, to celebrate, they went for a long walk, discussing not only their finances, but a casual observer would have had a strong suspicion that they loved one another. Any such suspicion would have been accurate. The street they'd chosen to walk was one of the safer ones in the area. Nevertheless, they quickened their pace as they went by Grizzly's Pub where the music was loud, and the drunken shouts were louder. When they got back to their 150 ft.^{2} living space in the basement, they treated themselves to pistachio ice cream and a few Oreo cookies.

Next morning, while they were still preparing to leave for work after a quick breakfast, the upstairs phone rang. Frankie called down to them and they both quickly climbed the stairs to the main floor. It was, indeed, Darius. "I've got great news for you guys! May I come over to your place when you get back from work today? I know you've got to head for work now, and I also know that you must be sitting on pins and needles, awaiting to hear the news. I just wanted to let you know that you can go through this day of work without a load of uncertainty on your minds. If it's alright with you, I'll be down around 7 PM." "Of course, we will be waiting with bated breath for whatever news you have," they both responded, almost in unison. They heard a faint chuckle as Darius wished them a good day.

That day was Wednesday, and it proved to be memorable in more ways than one. At the accounting office, everything was proceeding in a normal fashion until about 11 AM. Clients were being clients, and accountants were being accountants, the receptionist was doing her 'recepting', and Mr. Scrivens was doing his managerial responsibilities with his usual exactitude. At almost exactly 11 o'clock many, except for the hard-of-hearing CPA, Mr. Higgins, heard a wild spitting and hissing outside the main entrance. The receptionist ran to the front window where she could see everything that was happening, and there she saw not only a hissing cat, but also viewed another animal, commonly referred to as a 'polecat' in rural areas, sporting an upraised tail. They seemed to be facing off against one another. "Facing off" may not be strictly accurate in terms of the skunk's positioning, as it was actually backing up towards the cat. The receptionist, feeling sorry for the "poor kitty", opened the door just a crack, and the cat rushed into the building. By this time a small crowd had gathered, wondering what all the commotion was about. However, they quickly scattered when they realized that they had a significant problem on their hands. The polecat had won the battle outside, and the "poor kitty" turned out to be a feral cat and, as the popular old advertisement had proclaimed, "Never touched by human hands." Now they had a dual problem. Not only did they have a saber-toothed multi-clawed cat unhesitatingly prepared to dismember anyone who may have had the self-destructive presumption to accost it, but they had a malodorous emanation in the building of which they might never rid themselves. Not bothering to take the elevator, the frenzied wild cat rushed up the stairs to the second floor taking three or four steps at a time. Within less than a minute, the tabby had explored, very briefly, every office, leaped up on some of the desks and, in the process, distributed official documents across the floors. Some of the documentation even found its way into wastepaper baskets. One important parchment was not located until months later. It had found its way into the space between a closed drawer and the back of Cleo Washington's desk. Those people who had remained on the lower floor heard yells, screams, and some words not usually used in the precincts of such sedate surroundings. The cat, although having lived on the streets all its life and familiar with every possible danger in its usual habitat, appeared totally befuddled with the lack of any means of egress from this massive enclosure. Possibly attracted by a vague aroma of edibles, it found its way into the lunchroom, from where further shrieks were heard when the cat leaped onto the table and grabbed a fresh piece of ham before vaulting the 8 feet onto the shrouded window where it brought down the rod and its associated curtain in a heap on top of itself. Being highly resourceful, it quickly extricated itself and, with the slice of ham still in its mouth, found a corner next to the refrigerator where, with much guttural growling designed to ward off any reckless interloper, it enjoyed its repast and calmed down considerably with food in its belly and immediate danger apparently dissipated. It is probably needless to indicate that the two ladies who had been having their lunch left both their lunch and the room quickly … in fact, they moved rather more swiftly than they had in their track and field events some ten or thirty years ago (one never knows with women as they maintain themselves so well). However, wherever they went, the aroma went with them. The exterminator was called. He and his newly acquired apprentice arrived. A merry chase ensued (resulting in a short visit to the local emergency room for the apprentice who, incidentally, sought other employment opportunities next day), and the cat was removed, but the smell was not. The next day was a paid vacation for all employees as Cinder Clear Restoration (they'd branched out and were seriously considering a change of name … possibly to something like "NoMoreStench") was, on Melody's recommendation, called in to rid the building of the odor of the rather odious, but well-meaning, mammal. After all, the innocent skunk had simply been doing all it could to protect itself and its young. (Later, an inconspicuous tree trunk hollow with three cute offspring was discovered not 30 feet from the back entrance to the prestigious business office). It had been just another fun day at Windy City Financial Services. At least, it was considered that in later years as the story was told … and retold … sometimes being considerably embellished for the benefit of later employees.

When Melody picked Horatio up at the school about 6:15 PM that evening, she couldn't wait to tell the story of what happened at her workplace. She had sprayed herself liberally with cologne and was feeling quite presentable for her husband. However, the moment he opened the passenger door, he reeled backwards, saying, "Did you just drive over a skunk?" For a moment she sat there, nonplussed, wondering how he could mistake her Eau de Toilette for the stench of the mercaptan spray of "that stinky reptile" (as one of the women diners in the lunchroom had referred to it). But she quickly realized there was no way she could hide the truth. She told him the whole story.

She did not expect his stunned reply. "I can't believe it! I also had the weirdest experience at school today. It was nothing as wild as your story, but, in my books, it was also, to say the least, out of the ordinary. Just after you dropped me off at school this morning, as always, I was on my way to my office to put on the usual coveralls. But before I got there, as I was walking past the principal's office, I saw a number of people, most of whom were dressed casually as I am now, I heard one of the ladies in the group say, "That's him – he fits the description Principal Radner gave us. He sure got here quickly." I was a bit surprised, and I asked them if there was something I could do for them. That same lady … the one who had obviously clothed herself with more finesse than most … responded with, "Principal Radner told us he was going to ask you to give us a tour of the school." I had given one or two individuals tours in the past, but I was a bit surprised that I would be asked to give a tour to a group of 15 or 16 people. Of course, I offered, "I'll be glad to give you a tour." Every one of them was informally attired, and I naturally surmised that they were janitors and custodians from other schools or colleges. So, I gave them the grand tour. Initially, I took them to my small office and its adjoining stockroom where I store chemicals and cleaning supplies of all kinds. It was a tight squeeze, but everybody was able to get in. Of course, I explained to them that this was actually a restricted area, but I assumed they all had the necessary clearance to visit it. I proceeded to show them our well-stocked shelves of trisodium phosphate, peracetic acid, and glutaraldehyde. I told them that we were temporarily out of quaternary ammonium compounds, but that, while they had been ordered long ago, there'd been a mix-up at the supplier's end; the products were, fortunately, expected any day now. I explained to them how diatomaceous earth was my all-time favorite for absorbing chemical spills and, not to monopolize the conversation, I asked them what they used. I was quite surprised when there was dead silence and strange looks exchanged between my guests. Not wanting to embarrass them, as they were obviously here to learn, I led by example, "Let's go into the crawlspace. There's something there I want to show you regarding our ingenious water supply system, as well as how our school's architect designed our sewage system to operate most effectively." At this point an imposing gentleman, who appeared to be the spokesman, intervened in the procedure, "Before you take us into your crawlspace … I'm sure it's most enlightening … and then on to the boiler room, I fear there's been a misunderstanding here. As interesting as the information is that you have been sharing with us, it was not our intention to learn about your cleaning compounds and sewer system. You see, I'm the Minister of Education for the State of Illinois, these two are my aides, and the rest of our group are superintendents from the various school districts in the greater Chicago area. We came to visit your school because it is the second most successful in producing thriving graduates, not only in South Chicago, but in the entire city." Then, with a smile as wide as all outdoors on his handsome black face, he sincerely thanked me for the tour, then informed all of us of his intention: 'I can't wait to tell the governor of our experience here today!' I read somewhere that there are at least 15 shades of red; doubtlessly I displayed every one of them."

Melody had expected all along that there would be this kind of an ending to Horatio's story. That, no doubt, explained why she had been trying to hide her giggling as Horatio was relating the embarrassing account to her. Then, in spite of himelf, he joined in with her, not only because of the unbelievable experience, but just because he loved seeing her giggle. She was so fun-loving, and Horatio knew they would be telling and retelling that story as the years rolled on. No doubt it would also be making the rounds in the state legislature. Maybe this experience would turn out to be his five minutes of fame. Horatio hoped that it wouldn't be on the 6 o'clock news. If that happened, he may have had to find where Melody's feral cat hid during most of its daylight hours. To himself, Horatio mused, "I'm good with cats ... maybe it would accept me.

They'd almost forgotten about Darius. "We'll have to hurry with supper, dear," Melody observed when they realized what the time was. "We have only an hour … I guess it will be pork 'n beans and fried eggs again." "Fine with me," rejoined Horatio. They 'booted it' home as fast as the potholed streets allowed. On arrival, after stopping briefly for four large cans of tomato juice at the corner deli, they arrived at their abode. Donning one of Melody's aprons, Horatio got to work on the fine cuisine they had discussed earlier. Meanwhile, Melody, as the 19th century authors used to say, 'betook herself' to her parents' shower where she slathered yourself with the tomato juice, rinsed herself off, and went back to the basement, having shed much of the polecat smell. By the time she got to their "kitchenette", as she liked to call it, Horatio had the eggs fried to her liking and the beans piping hot and seasoned to his liking. The half loaf of 10-grain bread that Annabelle had sent down with Horatio made a fit addition to the simple meal.

At precisely 7 PM the doorbell rang, and Darius was welcomed by Frankie. "The kids told us that you were coming, so please come into our living room. There's a whole lot more room up here than in their crowded quarters downstairs. They'll be up in a minute." Frankie introduced Annabelle who, Darius thought, looked somewhat wan but, of course, that may have been her natural coloring. Annabelle offered Darius coffee, and he gratefully accepted with, "One cream, please." By the time Melody and Horatio had reached the top of the stairs, Annabelle was just bringing into the living room a steaming cup for their guest. As her parents were leaving the room, both young people again, almost simultaneously, assured them, "Don't go – there's nothing secret here!" Melody's parents appeared pleased that they had been invited to sit in on the discussion.

Darius immediately began with, "As I indicated to you this morning, I believe I have good news for you. The rental unit that we're talking about is a fully furnished apartment. I think you'll like the furniture, Melody. It's hardly ostentatious, nor is it what some people would call gauche. The previous renters are moving to Denver and didn't want to hire a moving van for just a few pieces of five-year-old furniture. They even left their 36-inch flatscreen television as it is attached to the wall. One of the big advantages of this particular apartment block is that each unit has its own washer and dryer. I know you will like that, Melody. The fridge and stove, although 10 years old, are in good working order. The kitchen is a bit cramped but does have what I would call ample storage area. Horatio, you have been by that apartment block many times, so you know that there is no inside parking. But you will also have noticed that there is ample outside parking, even if you have visitors. I know you're waiting for the bottom line – I'm getting there. But," he added with a smile, "I'm a salesman, and I need to tell you what you're getting for the money you spend."

"You already know that Wigglesworth had lowered his asking price to $850 per month. Landlords always add a little more than absolutely necessary to the monthly rent because they know, from bitter experience, that many renters are financially unstable. Because of the screening process that we employ, he's had very few bad experiences. But he has gone through a few ordeals some years ago.

When I described to him the wisdom that the two of you have shown in your financial planning, he agreed to come down to $825 per month. During our previous talk, I already told you that the price includes all utilities. The new information that I'm giving you today has to do with that slightly lower monthly cost and the fact that you will be renting a fully furnished apartment."

Without hesitation, Horatio immediately responded, "We'll take it!" Melody, ever the more careful one, took three more seconds before she responded with a resounding "Yes!" The die was cast. Out came the papers from Darius's briefcase. At this point Françoise and Annabelle withdrew to the kitchen while names were signed to the necessary documents, the still half-full cups having been carefully moved to make room on the coffee table. Moving day would be one week from today. That would make it exactly 5 ½ months that they had lived in the basement of Melody's parent's home. Annabelle, closely followed by Frankie, now entered the living room carrying a tray loaded with dainties. Melody's father brought in cans of Coca-Cola and 7-Up. As he set them down on the coffee table in front of Horatio, with a smile on his face and a twinkle in his eye, he whispered loudly enough for all to hear, "Well, we're finally able to get rid of you!" And, with a similar twinkle in his eye, Horatio responded with, "We couldn't wait to get out of here!"

Since the young couple, now married almost 6 months, had very few possessions, they didn't need to order a U-Haul to move a few changes of clothing, a few dishes, pots and pans, and Horatio's violin that had been passed down through four generations. Horatio had always intended to take lessons but had never gotten around to doing so. But he cherished the instrument dearly, knowing that his great-grandfather had played it in a small orchestra so many years ago.

A new chapter in their lives was about to begin. It promised variety.

CHAPTER 14

LIFE'S VICISSITUDES (OR) THE ROLLERCOASTER

In Melody's senior "Lit class", the soon-to-graduate students had been asked by their teacher, Sophie Quillington, to write a short 4-line couplet as a thoughtful personal guide for their futures. Melody had given an entire evening's thought to the small project, and had come up with this little snippet of wisdom:

> The journey winds through shadow and sun, Moments of joy and battles hard won.

> For life's ups and downs weave a tapestry rare, In every twist and turn resilience we wear.

Ms. Sophie (as she'd asked the students to call her) had given Melody a B+ for her work, and had observed, "Melody, your poem wouldn't qualify for a grant from the Guggenheim Foundation, but your mature grasp of reality is remarkable for a person of your age."

She'd then gone on to relate a personal story about her grandparents, a rare black couple in Germany during the late 30's … persecuted by Hitler, and literally driven out of their country in which they'd been born … then emigrating to New York, later moving to Chicago where her grandfather had "started over", setting up a shoe repair and footwear store. Ms. Sophie's father had expanded the business, eventually making it a thriving enterprise. "Bad times and good times are all part of life's tapestry … just as you described in your little poem, Melody."

The encouragement from Ms. Sophie for Melody's poem served as a frequent reminder, reinforcing her already innate understanding that life is not a serene river flowing with unending happiness.

The excitement of moving day was muted. One of the two chairs from their basement dwelling had, somehow, freed itself from its constraints in the open trunk, and tumbled onto the street when the Chevrolet hit a pothole. Horatio, although very handy, saw little point in attempting reparation of 23 smashed, but still recognizable pieces, in addition to the abundance of splinters that were left on the roadway. Although cause for some lamentation, that event paled in comparison to the phone call Annabelle had received from her doctor that very morning. The tests ordered by Dr. Nadia Gentille had indicated Stage 2 lung cancer. The family now realized the cause of Annabelle's wan appearance and seeming shortness of breath, even while she bravely attempted to appear totally normal.

Later that day, the young couple was looking forward to welcoming family to the first evening in their new home; Melody, of course, had guided Horatio's efforts in arranging … and rearranging … the furniture to her liking. There'd been few words exchanged during the process. Frankie had provided Horatio with some advice on the subject … such as "Don't fight it, Son, you won't win!" On cue, their guests arrived. Frankie, Annabelle, and Emily (who shyly introduced Brad Parnell) looked on thoughtfully as the young couple gave them the 'tour' of their new home, but the conversation was stilted. A cloud had definitely cast a shadow on their celebratory plans for the evening. Before they'd received the sad news, Horatio had asked Pastor Wilfred and Kari Williams to join them at 8 PM for "a sort of dedication" of their apartment. Pastor Wilfred did share a quiet time with them, but his comments were not directed solely to the young couple and their new living quarters. The Lacostes received some of the attention as well. Somehow, the root beer floats were not quite as tasty as Horatio had anticipated them to be. The pastor and his wife were the first ones to say their goodbyes; all three parents and Brad left shortly thereafter, knowing that "the kids" would want to have the rest of the evening to themselves.

Their guests having left, the young couple, over the sink while washing dishes, conversed in tones that were, initially, quietly serious. But then, Horatio dropped one of the Melmac saucers on the floor; with remarkable precision it negotiated its way around the corner and, from there, found its way into the living room. Then, like a whirling dervish, circling quickly, made its own valiant attempt at performing perpetual motion. This unusual feat executed by an inanimate object struck them both as hilarious. Of course, Melody's giggle started it all.

The excitement of a new home, combined with the foreboding news they'd received about Annabelle, augured against any possibility of sleeping in. The next day was a Saturday, and the new apartment dwellers received an unannounced visit from Darius Thompson and Odell Wigglesworth. The first words from Darius were, "I hope we are not intruding, but I've told Odell here so much about you; he smilingly commented that he had to, and I quote, 'wiggle my way into their lives.'" Melody's giggle was quickly stifled. Introductions were made, and Melody hastened to get her French press into action. Coffee was served, and the most convivial conversation ensued. Odell was definitely not some austere individual often characterized (and occasionally justified) as "slumlord" by some members of the media. He turned out to be a very companionable character who loved a good laugh, often at his own expense. "Since you opened the subject," inquired Horatio, "do you know how your ancestors acquired your rather unusual last name?" In response, Odell told a couple of stories about his less than dignified surname. He had Melody giggling in no time. Upon hearing Melody's giggle, Odell with a chuckle of his own, observed in a loud whisper to Horatio, "Are you sure your wife's maiden name isn't 'Gigglesworth'?" At this question, Melody's giggling turned into helpless laughter from which she was unable to extricate herself for a significant period of time. Her mirth did not subside much, if at all, when Odell felt it was appropriate to continue. Nor was Melody the only one who found the conversation amusing.

"There are actually a number of legends about the surname Wigglesworth." At this point, everyone heard yet another quickly squelched giggle. Odell smiled and went on. "One of the family legends goes something like this: Back in medieval times there was a knight by the name of Sir Reginald, apparently the first black knight in history. When I first heard this legend, I had to suspend disbelief as it is very unlikely that a slave would have become a knight. There is, however, a rumor that "Sir Morien the Moor' was a black knight in King Arthur's court. Apparently, as the story goes, Sir Reginald was known throughout the kingdom for his uncanny ability to squirm out of any precarious situation. Sort of an old-time Houdini. Whether it was escaping from an angry dragon's lair or slipping away from a tyrant king's wrath, Sir Reginald's knack for wiggling his way to safety earned him the admiration of all who knew him. It was even rumored that he had rescued a pretty damsel from the clutches of an evil knight who had imprisoned her in an almost impenetrable labyrinth beneath his formidable castle. His escapades became so legendary that people started referring to him as 'Wiggle-worth,' a title that stuck with his descendants through the ages." For some reason, this almost believable story resulted in a fresh spasm of giggles from over somewhere near where yet more coffee was being prepared.

"Although there are a number of other theories about my surname's history," he continued, "I'll only mention one other one. Apparently, somewhere in the 1300s, during the reign of King Edward I, there was a jester in the king's court who was known only as 'Chester the Jester'. He became renowned for his bizarre yet highly entertaining dance moves. He would wiggle and twist his body in ways that mesmerized crowds at village festivals as well as in the courtroom of the king. He was double-jointed and, many believed, possibly even triple jointed. Inevitably, people began referring to him as Chester Wigglesworth. And, Chester was no dummy. He knew that his newly assigned surname would bring in a lot more shekels than 'Chester Smith'. This story is actually more believable than the first piece of folklore; there are actual records of black jesters in the courts of kings and noblemen."

Before their guests left, Melody and Horatio knew that they had two new friends. Sure, they'd done business with them, but the nature of the conversation had drawn them all under the comfortable dome of companionship. "Thank you for the coffee, folks. We certainly did not intend to stay as long as we did, but the visit has been wonderful, and we wish you the very best in your new digs," offered Odell. As he turned to leave, Darius gave the young couple a thumbs-up.

CHAPTER 15

THE BUSINESS OF LIVING ... TO ITS CONCLUSION

Arthur Conan Doyle once wrote, "We may have learned something in that school of sorrow where some of our earthly lessons are taught." If not all of us, at least most of us, regardless of our station in life, have attended that same school. Some have referred to a similar institute, "The School of Hard Knocks". The marks received upon graduation vary considerably. In fact, those who benefit most from the education provided are often the ones who audit the course, watching the graduates who succeed as well as observing the dropouts.

Although the percentage of babies born into this world with silver spoons in their mouths is much higher than it was 250 or 300 years ago, by far the greater percentage are born with picks and shovels in their tiny expectant hands. Good times and troubled times are the lot of the rich and poor alike. Rev. Williams, at this point, would have quoted from the Scriptures, "The rain falls on the just and the unjust."

Annabelle's situation did not improve. She had occasional difficulty breathing, and her normal energy levels were way down. Further tests were initiated. Upon receiving Dr. Gentille's urgent call before 8 AM on a Tuesday morning some few months after her daughter's and son-in-law's move to Bluebird Apartments, Frankie took the day off work, driving Annabelle to her doctor's office. "I'm glad you came along as well, François. I will not mince any words. Your condition is very serious, Annabelle. Your cancer is spreading, and it is highly unlikely that the medical profession can help you. Barring a miracle of some kind, I cannot promise you even four months of life. Of course, we might be able to extend your life by a month or two with some mitotic inhibitors – those are drugs that stop cell division – but there would, almost certainly, be undesirable side effects."

The Lacostes had both been aware that Annabelle's situation was probably serious. However, as anyone who has gone through a similar experience can attest, the shock was still palpable. Neither one responded with desperate demands that more be done. They knew that the wise and resourceful doctor had done everything she could in terms of study and research of the situation. They also knew that she had majored in oncology and could have been a specialist but had, instead, chosen family practice.

All of which is not to say that tears were not shed. Even the kind doctor reached for her facial tissues. And used them. "Please take some time to talk with each other and with your family. Let me know – soon – if you want me to prescribe the drug treatment. And, in the meantime, if you have any questions, or you just want to talk, please contact my office."

It was a cool day with intermittent light rain showers. As François helped his wife into her light jacket, she squeezed his hand and, standing on her tiptoes, whispered something into his ear that only he heard. It brought a smile to his lips and a teardrop below his right eye.

They waited until "the kids" returned from work before calling them. Attempting to ease into the bad news, Frankie, a forced smile in his voice, said to Horatio when he answered the phone, "We miss you. We want you back in our basement!" Then, with a catch, he added,

"Can you guys come over after your evening meal? We have something we need to share with you." "Is it about Annabelle?" asked Horatio. There was a short delay as Horatio heard a nose being blown and then, a subdued "Yes, very much so. But after she's shared her heart with you, I will also have something to say."

When the young couple arrived, they were welcomed with hugs. Before many words were exchanged, Kimberly-Clark benefited from the number of tissues used by four people who loved each other dearly. "Let me make the coffee, Mother," offered Melody. Since all four agreed that Melody made the best coffee of any of them (French press or traditional coffee maker), no one resisted her offer. "It's going to be decaf, but I'll make it really strong!" While the coffee was brewing, Melody rejoined the others. Frankie and Annabelle took turns, sharing what the doctor had told them.

Then followed comments from both Melody's parents – comments that stuck with Melody and Horatio for many years thereafter. Somehow, they both knew that the words they were about to hear would be weighty. Annabelle spoke first. Although the evidence of tears on her cheeks was obvious, her voice was strong as she shared her thoughts.

"Obviously today's news is shocking to you kids, but it's not entirely a surprise to me. I think even Frankie is more shocked than I am. I've suspected something like this for a while now. The only decision that has to be made – and I'd like you all to be part of it – is whether or not you think I should take that drug that may give me a few extra months of life. I know that, in the end, you'll all say it's my decision, but I'd still like to get your thoughts. I've known a lot of love from a lot of wonderful people in my 51 years of life. Whether we live 51 years or 101 years, life goes quickly. Obviously, from an emotional point of view, I want to stay around as long as possible. At the physical level, my body is obviously beginning to shut down. But at the spiritual level, I'm totally at peace, fully expecting an eternal life far superior to anything we can expect here." Then, struggling to breathe deeply for a few moments, she continued. "Please give me your honest thoughts as to what you think I should do. The question is simple. The decision will be final. Should I, or should I not, take that drug? After we left the doctor's office today, she did give me a short call, indicating that there have been instances where this drug gave the sufferer another whole year of life, but that it was almost always accompanied by ever-increasing pain."

A pin didn't drop, but if it had, all four would've heard it. Kimberly-Clark benefited yet again. Reactions were slow in coming.

For a long minute, there was no response. Then Horatio spoke. Slowly. Deliberately. "I'm the newest member of this family, and I've seen how incredibly much you love one another, and how that shared love radiates out to the world around you. Mom Annabelle, you and Frankie have raised a daughter who is beautiful in every way. You have invested your life in her, and that investment has paid off in so many ways. I'm trying to look at this in a commonsense way, but I don't know if I can do that. Life and death decisions do not constitute part of my repertoire of human experience. I couldn't have had a more wonderful mother-in-law than you. Obviously, I'd love to have you around to see your grandchildren graduate from college." At that point Horatio noticed the part teasing, part questioning, look in Annabelle's eyes. "No, Melody is not pregnant!" Everyone smiled at that, and Melody even threatened to commence one of her trademark giggles.

"Obviously, it's your decision, but if a few extra months means untold pain for you, it would be selfish of me to suggest taking the medicine."

"Your turn, my sweet daughter," voiced her mother. At that term of endearment Melody, as quick with tears as she was with giggles, sobbed, "I'm only trying to think of what's best for you, Mommy, and I have to agree with Horatio. I would so hate to see you suffer more than you must."

It was Frankie's turn. With a barely stifled sob in his voice, he quietly, and with bowed head, admitted, "Annabelle and I have already had a heartrending discussion about this, as you can imagine. The conclusion you both arrived at is also my wish for the wife of my dreams."

"Then it's settled," stated Annabelle, no hesitancy whatsoever in her voice. "I'll talk to the doctor tomorrow. Now," she voiced with enthusiasm, "let's have some of that pistachio ice cream that my favorite son-in-law likes so much!"

For the next half hour or so, it was like old times – not that the times were that old. The young couple entertained the middle-aged couple with hyperbolically embellished recollections of the recent escapades in their respective places of employment. The feral cat became a man-eating tiger, and the state dignitaries became world leaders, having just flown in from NATO meetings.

As spoons became less active in stirring cream and/or sugar in coffee cups, Horatio sensed, from the look in Frankie's eyes, that he had yet another subject on his mind. "Hey, Dad, you'd mentioned something about having a word to say to us after Mom had shared her news." "You're very perceptive, Son. Yes, I do have something to say."

"Obviously, it is self-evident that life can be uncertain. Mom and I had no inkling that one of us would be passing away before we'd been married even 30 years. Fortunately, and yet even that is sort of sad, we were reasonably wise in saving money and seeing it grow. However, honestly, we were going at it sort of hit and miss. My advice to both of you is to give even more thought to your investment plans. Don't just assume that everything will be alright if and when you get to your retirement years. Way back when I was hired by SparkTech in N'awlins, my immediate supervisor was a hard-working, fun-loving, guy by the name of Joe Welter. He was very good at his job, and very helpful in making me the well-respected 'circuit guy' people say I am today. In those days the company had no retirement plan for employees and, although they paid well, Joe liked his toys. He loved putting on his leather jacket and making 500-mile weekend round trips on his succession of Hondas and Harleys. It seemed he had a new motorcycle every year or two. The last bike I remember him buying cost more than most cars at the time. As for saving for a rainy day or for his eventual retirement, that was always for another day. Even though he was in his mid to late 30s at the time, he'd always say that he wanted to enjoy life while he was still young. Long story short, he had his fun but, when the company went belly up, he was without work for over a year. He ran out of money, sold his 'cycle for less than half what he paid for it, and is now living in low-income housing. I guess the only good thing about it is that the guy he went biking with lives in the same housing complex. In fact, before we left what tourists call 'the big easy', I wanted to say goodbye to Joe, and to thank him once again for the good start he gave me. The groundskeeper directed me to where Joe and his buddy were seated on a park bench. As I approached from behind them, I heard them reminiscing about their biking days. Last I heard, Joe, now in his early 60s, did have a job working part-time in a small shop specializing in refurbishing motorcycles." Frankie stopped for a moment, sipped his now cold coffee, and continued. "As you can tell, there will be a point to this story. Annabelle and I have set aside a specific portion of our income every year. We have a few bonds, but most of our savings are in low interest bank deposits. Over the past few years, the interest has averaged around 3%. That may have been sufficient for a very modest retirement. But since those early days, I realized we could have done a lot better. Now," and he paused for another sip, "I know you are setting aside a significant portion of your incomes for a house as well as for your eventual retirement, and I commend you for that. But here's my advice for you: find a highly reputable investment firm with a solid track record – do your research – and invest much, if not most, of your savings with them. Such a firm can invest in blue-chip companies and successful corporate entities where the dividends they provide can be reinvested year after year. Then, watch your money grow."

At this point Melody started to raise her hand, almost as if she was still in school, and interrupted her father. "But, Dad, aren't all those corporations just out to make money for themselves? There is so much in the news about 'greedy corporations', and sometimes we hear about a lot of dishonesty and even criminal actions by the CEOs and other bigwigs. Should we really be supporting such organizations with our heart-earned savings?"

Frankie, almost absentmindedly, brought his coffee cup to his lips again, and only then realized his cup was empty. Melody started to rise to her feet, but her father signaled to her to remain seated. "I don't need any more coffee, and even though your decaf is pretty good, I don't really want any more. Yes, my dear, to a point you are right. As in every other walk of life, there are good guys and there are bad guys. There are low level street hoodlums and there are silk-suited corporate moguls who know how to steal much more money than the street hoods. That's why it is so incredibly important to get the right financial advisor. And," he paused as if wondering how to emphasize what he was about to say, "do it sooner than later!"

Then, almost as an afterthought, Frankie added, "There is almost no individual with a startup company who thinks, 'Man, I can't wait to benefit all of society with the money my business makes.' People go into business for what amounts to selfish reasons; they want to get rich and be able to live their dream. But, remember this poorly understood reality … for every dollar made by a successful corporation, many times that amount goes right back into the rest of society. I read a book by a guy who, after years of research, demonstrated conclusively - that one dollar of corporate profit generates eight dollars for the economy! That $8 goes into employing tens of thousands of people, building communities with all the associated goods and services, as well as constructing roads, hospitals, schools, universities, and paying the teachers, professors, doctors, and nurses … all from taxes collected because many different entrepreneurs had 'dreams'. And, kids, here's the 'kicker': the money you invest in those financially solid companies … it's those companies which will end up providing you with your retirement income."

Needless to say, that night Melody and Horatio were not asleep by their usual 11:15 PM. For some time, they were both thinking their own thoughts. Finally, Horatio quietly spoke, "Wow, this has been quite a day. First, we were dealing with your mother's traumatic news, and then your dad gave us solid advice about our financial future. That's quite the 'juxtaposition' – I couldn't wait to use that word – I heard Principal Radner use it last week." Melody smothered a slight, almost hesitant, giggle. Horatio continued, "We've got a lot to think about but, as soon as we can, I think we need to make an appointment with that Isabella Chavez lady who was recommended to us."

CHAPTER 16

PATH TO THE RAINBOW'S END

Despite their best intentions, life got in the way, and the call to Great Lakes Financial Stewards didn't happen, either the next day or even the next week. Finally, after some gentle prompting by Horatio, Melody made the call. Since it was Mr. Scrivens who had advised Melody to touch base with Ms. Chavez, and because Melody had already spoken with the head "steward" on the phone, Horatio felt it would be appropriate for her to call as there was a connection; it certainly wouldn't be a cold call.

Melody's call was answered on the second ring – no music played, and there was no message saying, "We are receiving more calls than normal, please hold." A very pleasant-sounding female voice with a noticeable southern accent answered, "Hey there, y'all! You've got Great Lakes Financial Stewards on the li-en. Who can I send your wa-ay?" Some of the "stewards" at Great Lakes had expressed their initial concern about Stella Wilkinson's (to whom the pleasant-sounding female voice belonged) "drawl", thinking it didn't sound sufficiently professional for such an august organization. However, clients, both male and female, so enjoyed her many and varied telephone greetings, management and stewards alike realized Stella was actually, at least partially, responsible for an increase in business.

With the usual smile in her voice, Melody asked to speak to Isabella Chavez. Stella, in her own inimitable fashion, responded with, "Oh, Sugar, I'm sorry but ya gotta go talk to one of the underling stewards, not the head steward." (Stella was also known to have responded in a number of other enjoyable, albeit surprising, ways. One of the stewards, passing by the receptionist desk, had heard her say to a potential client who had also wanted to talk to Ms. Chavez, "Well, butter my biscuit! I reckon y'all will havta taw-ak to someone further down the li-en.").

However, when Melody informed Stella that Mr. Anthony "Tony" Scrivens of Windy City Financial Services had referred her to Ms. Chavez, and that she herself had spoken with Ms. Chavez, the southern belle (who was now 48 years old), brightly reacted with, "A'hm so sorry, dearie, a'hl put y'all ray-at through. Thank ya for callin' Greyat La-iks." Melody smiled, enjoying the fact that Stella was "spreading it thick" with that delightful southern lilt. Melody decided it couldn't be called a drawl, because it sounded far too musical to be called that.

Isabella Chavez employed a personal gatekeeper for her calls. When Isabella was deeply in conversation with a client who hung onto her every word, only a tornado or a fire would have allowed afro-chic Maya Lee to interrupt their conversation. As it happened, however, Isabella was between meetings and, when Maya told her it was Melody Jefferson, Isabella immediately reached for the phone. "I've been expecting a call from you – Tony and I were talking just the other day. He requested that I deal with you directly when you called."

"I know both you and your husband – Horatio, right? – are working. He's a janitor, I'm told. And you're sort of an understudy at Windy City. Because of the great relationship we enjoy with Scrivens' organization, I'm glad to personally help you. Over the years, he has sent us numerous clients who, I'm happy to say, are happy with our stewardship of their finances. I know from ongoing conversations with him that he has a special place in his heart for the two of you. Not only that, but one of his long time CPAs, one Cedric Ravenshadow, has spoken very highly of you. Can you come to our office (and here she briefly consulted Maya) next Tuesday at 5:30 PM?" Hearing Melody's positive response, Isabella continued, "Bring all your financial details with you, no matter how insignificant they seem to be. I need to see absolutely everything that has anything to do with money. That includes your budget, your income, your taxes paid, any investments that you have and, of course, your latest bank statements. And, in the next day or two, email me a summary of everything you're going to show me on Tuesday. By the way, I'm having you come in at the end of the workday because I want to spend as much time with you as necessary so I can get you guys on the right track as quickly as possible. Now, I'm sorry to have to go, another client is coming in through the doorway, but I look forward to meeting both of you next Tuesday."

Horatio was the epitome of the average guy who, although by no means careless with his financial documents, would occasionally wonder where he had left a particular statement. He never forgot where he'd last used his favorite Phillip's screwdriver, but it was not unusual for him to misplace his wallet. He had realized quickly that Melody should be the one to look after the books. He often marveled at her meticulous attention to detail.

Over the next few days, amidst their ongoing concern for Annabelle's situation and the family trauma it had created, Melody collected all the relevant financial information that Ms. Chavez had requested. Melody even went so far as to bring in receipts for virtually everything they had purchased so far this year.

"Tuesday at 5:30 PM" arrived quickly. Melody and Horatio arrived equally quickly – actually 10 minutes early – at the workplace of the "stewards". That unusual designation for 'financial advisors' had prompted the couple to do some research concerning the word "steward". One of the many definitions was "a fiscal agent employing expertise in managing the financial affairs of a client." Great Lakes had 15 such "stewards" on their staff. They never employed unseasoned advisors. Due to their reputation, there were many young, enthusiastic, newly graduated gals and guys from university commerce departments and business schools who applied for work with them, but the Great Lakes HR man, Boris Shorochevsky, in his never-totally-lost Russian accent, always told them, "Go get experience elsevere, den come back us in five to sefen years. Bring your client provit/loss statements wid you. Den we consider takin' look at you."

Isabella Chavez immediately made the young couple completely at ease. A steaming cup of strong coffee was placed before Horatio and an equally potent decaf before Melody. Ms. Chavez had done her homework. Among her first words of greeting were, "Please call me Isabella – just because I'm much older than you doesn't mean that you need to be in awe of me."

Isabela had before her the one-page summary that Melody had emailed to her. "Give me a minute to just refresh my memory," she asked. Melody and Horatio watched Isabella's large dark eyes scanning through their short documentation. Then, she slowly raised her head and, with a smile of what could only be interpreted as admiration, she shared her praise, "This is excellent – what a start! If what you've summarized here reflects what all those papers you've brought along suggests, I can see that most of our time today will be devoted to how we can make your savings grow even more quickly. I like the way you have joint accounts for everything and how you've divided those housing and retirement savings into separate accounts. Together, you've been making a more than adequate income to allow for a comfortable, but modest, lifestyle while still setting aside significant funds for your longer-term goals. I see that your medium-term goal is to have your own house within the next decade and a half. You'll still need a mortgage, but it will not be by any means prohibitive. There are very few couples of your age who deliberately set aside money for retirement. It's great being young, but – if only we, at 25, had the accumulated wisdom of older people. And, we older people, needless to say, would love to have the enthusiasm, not to say anything of the looks, we had when we were younger! But that's another subject," she smiled. "Tony (as she always referred to Anthony Scrivens) has also told me that you, Melody, may want to be a stay-at-home Mom if and when children begin to make their appearance. You will obviously not be able to put as much money into your savings at that point, but it's a life decision for which I have much respect. My husband and I have never been able to have children – we've done very well financially, but I know we have missed out on some of life's most cherished experiences. There are so many factors to weigh when it comes to making a decision to be with your children or to work outside the home. I often feel sorry for young couples nowadays. Living is expensive and the decisions can be very difficult. Just a word of advice to you, Melody. There are various ways in which you can combine being at home with your children while enjoying the excitement – and the challenge – of a home-based business. But that's a decision for the future."

"You two are here today because you want to investigate ways of increasing the return on your savings and investments. In today's economic climate, it is difficult to truly put money aside for retirement when you're getting 3% interest on your savings while, at the same time, the inflation rate is anywhere between 2% and 5%. The long and short of it is that you need to investigate financial instruments that will return significantly higher earnings. And there are a number of excellent ways of doing just that."

"Let me give you some very basic information so that there will be no misunderstandings whatsoever. Number one: there are no guarantees when you make an investment. No serious investment counsellor will ever guarantee even a bottom-line percentage return on your investment. Of course, human nature being what it is, there are many shysters out there who will 'guarantee' you a return of 15% every year. And I'm not even talking about those who guarantee 50% a month! If anyone ever tells you some unbelievable story about incredible returns, either they are lying through their teeth – or – they're missing the teeth through which they are lying. Many of these folks, if not dining behind bars at the public's expense or recovering from blows inflicted by their clients, are hiding out in Borneo. Here at "Stewards" we are totally open about the returns our clients receive."

At this point, Maya, as if on cue, brought in three small folders, one of which she handed to each of the three people in the room. She also brought back two coffee pots with which she warmed up the half full cups. Isabella continued, "This is the documentation we've asked our auditors to provide for us so that we can share with our clients and potential clients the actual performance of the investments with which they have entrusted us. We could go into a lot more detail describing returns from various individual stocks and bonds, and a plethora of other investment strategies and instruments. But what this document shows you is the actual return on investment in every one of the 32 years we've been in existence. You'll quickly notice that the lowest annual return was actually a minus figure. In that particular year our clients lost 3.9% of their savings. By the way, that was the year that the average national percentage loss was 11.4 %. The lowest positive return was 0.5%, as you can see. Now, you will also note that our highest annual return was 23.7%. Overall, through those 32 years, our clients have increased their financial holdings by 8.2 % on an annual basis."

Melody caught herself, about to ask a question. Perceptively, Isabella asked her what she was about to say. "I was going to say," Melody paused, then volunteered, "Some time ago I would probably have mimicked some of those TV people who are always talking about how evil those millionaires are, taking from the poor to live their lavish lifestyles. I would have asked – aren't many of those financial instruments basically just supporting greedy corporations? But then, I remembered what Dad stressed. If I remember correctly, I will paraphrase him, 'Profit is a truly honorable and legitimate goal. While, given the nature of humanity, the profit motive can lead to greed, that profit goes back into society, multiplying the positive effect that dollars can make for so many necessary purposes … including, by the way, what will, one day, be your retirement income!' Dad told me he learned all this way too late in life."

"Your father was obviously a wise man, but he discovered the power of compounding interest much later than he should have – these things just aren't taught in school as much as they should be. If they were, we'd probably have a lot fewer people in dire circumstances when they wished to retire."

"Now, having gone through the documents you've provided, I see you have already accumulated a nest egg, even though it might be more accurately termed a hummingbird's nest egg! I've seen enough of the great information you have provided to make some recommendations. First, my recommendation to you, based on your age, would be a combination of blue-chip companies and a few slightly riskier companies that have been thoroughly vetted by our analysts. Later in life, as you approach middle-age (and it happens quickly, I assure you) you can always back away from some of the riskier options, but that will be your call."

"Now, young people, I'm going to do some simple mathematical gymnastics with you. I want you to have a clear picture of what regular saving and investing can do for you. Here goes:

First, let's make a few assumptions – let's assume that you start saving at age 25. I know you're 25 right now, Horatio, and between the two of you you've already begun saving substantial percentages of your income, setting aside a specific amount every month. That 'every month' is powerful and I'll show you why. Let's also assume a retirement age goal of 65 years – that's 40 years from now. Now, I've already told you that we've been successful in achieving an average of 8.2% annual return for our clients. But for our purposes today, let's go with the historical average for a well-managed diversified portfolio … it's 7%. Of course, there are many that earn less than that as there are those that earn more.

Many of the following points you already know, but I'm going to review them with you anyway. Here they are, in point form – and yes, I'll give you a copy of this information.

- Take advantage of employer-sponsored plans. Contribute enough to at least get the full employer match if available. This is essentially free money.

- You can also consider an individual retirement account (IRA). Such contributions are tax-advantaged, helping your savings grow faster.

- Aim for a minimum annual return of 7% over the long term. This may mean investing more heavily in stocks early on and gradually shifting to more conservative investments as retirement approaches.

- As your income increases or expenses decrease (due to paying off your house mortgage, for example), increase your savings rate. In other words, invest more as your income increases.

- Avoid high fees and expenses wherever possible – we are here to help you with that.

- Stay disciplined – avoid withdrawing from retirement savings except for dire emergencies. Early withdrawals can incur penalties and will diminish long-term growth.

Now, while we all know that inflation is virtually inevitable, we also know that, if at age 65 you have accumulated a $1 million portfolio … don't look so shocked! … you will likely have an income of over $5800 per month. Most people can get by on that amount." Melody, with a whisper heard by the other two, reiterated with emphasis, "I guess!" Isabella smiled and commented, "Remember, Melody, $5800, in another 40 years, will not be worth what it is today. That's why it's so important to increase your retirement contributions as you go along in life. In 40 years, it's quite conceivable that you will need 10,000 or even $12,000 a month to live a comfortable life. We just don't know the future, no matter how we try to prognosticate."

"Let me be a mathematical gymnast for another moment. Over 40 years, contributing $300 per month, your contributions will have totaled $144,000. That sounds like a lot of money, and it is. But, because of what we often refer to as 'the miracle of compound interest', your

$144,000 contribution, by age 65, will have 'ripened' (as my uncle used to say) to a magnificent $1,040,000. And, remember that's at a 7% return per year. Obviously, an 8.2% return per year would raise that total significantly. Melody, you can do that math on your own … a simple 'ratio' will give you the answer." It took Horatio a moment longer than it took Melody to catch the play on words.

Isabella continued, "I'm going to send some information home with you, including the data I've shared with you this afternoon. If you do decide to invest with us, you can be assured beyond a shadow of any doubt, that we will work with your money as we would with our own. Depending on individual risk tolerance, we invest in the same financial instruments that we recommend to our clients. And, one last thing … if you wish to transfer your bank savings to a potential account with us, you are welcome to do so. That would give you a great head start, but don't feel pressured to do so. It's your money so it's your call."

Horatio responded, "Thank you very much for sharing your time and your expertise with us. We realize you went above and beyond the call of duty because of your business relationship with Anthony Scrivens. Mr. Scrivens has spoken so highly of you, not only in direct conversation with Melody, but Melody heard the same recommendation as she spent time with the various CPAs, especially so with Mr. Ravenshadow. We will take this information home, and I'm sure you will hear from us very soon."

As their Chevrolet seemed almost to guide them back to their apartment block on its own, the two young marrieds thought more of the future than of the past. With a note of melancholy in her voice, Melody observed, "Mother's dying, and here we are talking of our financial situation 40 years from now. When one takes a step back from the immediacy of it all, for some reason, I'm reminded of a bit of poetry by Grantland Rice that my mother so often quoted to me." Horatio, equally somber, spoke, "Now you've got me interested in poetry rather than money – what is that bit of poetry?" In a lilting tone so appropriate for the words, Melody recited:

"The threads of the ages, the warp and the woof,
Are part of the pattern we weave through our youth;
And the way that we blend it will fashion the line
Of the pattern that's yours and the pattern that's mine."

CHAPTER 17

REFLECTIONS

After breakfasting on granola and stewed prunes, the elderly couple, with careful attention to avoid spilling their decaffeinated coffee, moved from their dining room table out to their fifth-floor patio overlooking South Padre Island beach with the ocean's never ceasing waves rolling into shore. Setting down their cups on the small but functional sideboard, they carefully lowered themselves to their comfortable all-weather beach chairs and, cozily seated, breathed in the invigorating sea air. Totally at ease in each other's presence, no words were spoken for at least 10 minutes. The weather grew warmer, and the coffee grew cooler, but neither man nor woman stirred, either to cool off in their condo or to warm up their coffee.

They reveled in each other's presence as they watched a Monarch butterfly flitting about, occasionally dropping down to lower levels to examine a flower it hadn't noticed on its earlier excursion for nectar. Even the raucous seagulls, coming from north and south and beating vigorous wings, almost too close to a little boy who was throwing them popcorn, didn't disturb their reverie. Further to the north a family was enjoying the semitropical conditions; the 10-year-old boy was implementing an extensive engineering project, attempting to bring ocean water into a sandy reservoir some 20 feet upslope from the water's edge. The older child, a 12 or 13-year-old girl, was doing cartwheels and backflips. Although they were too far away to prove their theory, the elderly couple imagined they could see the smiles of approval on the faces of the children's parents.

They continued watching as a young Marine arrived for his daily morning exercise. He came out here once or twice every year for what he called "an intensive workout week". They watched him admiringly as he skipped rope in the soft sand for minute after endless minute. Then, in each hand, he picked up what must have been 20-pound weights, arcing them over his head and lowering them all the way down to the sand as he bent his knees and rose to do it all over again. Along came a young woman, running at a gracefully loping stride that was somewhere between a sprint and an energetic jog. On various occasions, on one of their strolls on the beach, the senior couple had met both of these young people and had visited with them, trying to avoid interrupting them for too long. The young Marine was able to continue his exercises while visiting with them. And, the young woman, noticeably slowing down as she approached the Marine (who, apparently, didn't mind the attention of the statuesque redhead), had occasionally stopped her running to visit with them as well.

The petite 73-year-old woman, turning her sparkling eyes on her husband, reminisced, "Remember when?" Her husband, now 76, turned to her slowly, reached for her hand and, with eyes that betrayed only love, replied, "I remember." Their hearts were full. They realized how blessed they were as they recalled their own stirrings of attraction so many years ago, yet how it all remained so fresh in their minds.

It was at times like this, more frequent now than ever before, that they talked both about what had been and about what was yet to come.

It was usually Horatio who began the reminiscences. Once he started with one memory, inevitably Melody would bring up another.

"Remember when" always began these discussions. However, contrary to the usual situation, this time it was Melody who started with, "Dear, do you remember our frequent financial discussions during the latter stages of our courtship and our early marriage years? We were concerned about how we could afford a home, but that apartment served us so well for the years while we were saving money for a house."

Horatio chuckled, "As always, Melody, you are including yourself when you say things like that. I know perfectly well that it was always myself who was more on edge about finances than you were. You invariably had a much better handle on money than I did."

Melody, with that shyly appreciative expression Horatio loved so well, modestly observed, "Thank you Ratio, but we all have our strengths – mine happens to be numbers. Neither one of us would ever think of ourselves as being anything above middle class in terms of income, but we have really done well." With a slow nod, Horatio agreed. Then, with a sudden quick turn of his head, as if he had never thought of asking her this question before, he queried, "Do you have any idea how much money we've made in our lifetimes? I'm not talking about babysitting and lawnmowing jobs, but actual full-time employment."

With a little twinkle in her eye, she kissed his cheek and asked, "Why don't you guess?" Melody watched the wheels turning in Horatio's head and, after a long pause, he responded, "It's probably more than I think it is, so I'll try to guess on the high side. I'll say that, with my salary plus your salary in the early years before you quit the formal workplace, we've probably earned at least $1 million. How close am I?"

"Well, my love, you were right about one thing. Our combined income was indeed 'at least' $1 million." Then, with her trademark giggle, she requested that he guess again. When Horatio had guessed twice more, raising his estimate by $100,000 each time, and was still too low, he gave up. "Now you've got me really curious – how much income did we earn in our lifetimes?"

"Okay, I'll tell you but have another sip of the cold coffee so that you don't have a heart attack when you hear the answer!" Horatio obliged. "Not including any of the money I made at Windy City or working from home for 3 years with Olivia Brightwell in Creationary, and not including any of the money we made from our investments after our retirement …" Here Melody paused, partly because she wanted to clarify some anomalies that had occurred in Horatio's janitorial years, but hesitated mainly because she deliberately wanted to see her husband in suspense just a little longer.

Finally, not able to maintain the suspense any longer, she explained, "At the age of 21, you began with the salary of $23,400. Not long after that you became head janitor and your salary rose to $36,795. Thereafter, there were quite regular yearly increases averaging 3%. In your late 30s, there were two years without a salary increase and then a couple of years where there was just a 2% raise which was followed three years later with a 2.5% raise. There were three separate occasions on which your salary peaked at the highest level provided by the Board. There were also a few years later when there was either no increase, a minor cost-of-living increase … and there was even one year when your wage was cut by 3%. In the last years of your employment your salary again twice peaked at the maximum provided for the position. Here's the bottom line: You made $2,664,246 as janitor for the school. I'd planned to bring this subject into our discussion today … here is the proof." She brought out a piece of lined paper from the bottom of the coffee tray. A shocked silence ensued. Finally, Horatio commented, "I would never have guessed it was anywhere near that high. But, when one thinks about it, with deductions for local, state, and federal taxes along with home expenses in raising our two daughters … I can see where it makes sense. We have been blessed!"

Their reverie was interrupted by an almost stationary Cessna … probably a 182, Horatio thought … dragging a massive Geico banner against a strong prevailing south wind. Another minute passed before the roar of the seemingly struggling aircraft became sufficiently quiet to allow conversation. To compensate for the still-noisy plane, Horatio raised his voice and continued, "Remember how determined you were, despite that dear old Chevy finally breaking down, to keep us on track for that house we'd planned on for so long? You insisted we still make those monthly investments for our first home. Largely because of your 'business head', we were able to make that little bungalow on Elm our home for 18 years … or was it 19?"

"It was 21," Melody smiled.

Probably five more minutes passed into the world of bygones before Melody again spoke. "Remember when we got the beautiful surprise that, despite all the prognostications, Mom's cancer went into remission? Dr. Nadia was so wrong – she must have apologized to Mom and to us at least three times for giving us such a scare. She was simply going according to the best of her knowledge, conceding that the recovery was as close to a miracle as she'd ever seen. Remember how we could hardly believe that Mom lasted another 16 years, finally dying at 67 – and then it went so quickly. She was even blessed to see her grandchildren! Remember the smile on her face when she saw our whole family enter her hospice room just two days before she died? Horatio, it was so good of Emily and your amazing stepfather, Brad, to make the trip from West Bend to join us. I'll always remember Mom's words that first night as we shared our goodnights, 'Don't cry, I'll see you again.'

But we cried anyway. Yet she hung on almost another full day. She declined the offer to be fully sedated. And then, the next day, when we all thought she was about to leave us, she seemed to revive – her sense of humor came to the fore as she, in an unexpectedly strong voice, asked me if her son-in-law had recently shown the United States president how ingeniously the Parkview School sewage system had been designed!" After all these years, Horatio still chuckled as he recalled his conscientious effort to afford the Illinois minister of education the opportunity now referred to by Annabelle.

A few re-lived embarrassed moments passed before Horatio rejoined, "But you're forgetting another, equally embarrassing situation in which you were involved, my dear Melody. You conveniently forgot that Annabelle, that next day, also recalled another story that had all of us in stitches. Remember when, while focusing on her grandchildren, and with her never-failing sense of humor, she recalled, 'There's also an interesting story about your mother, girls. One day, while she was busy at work at some accounting place – I can never remember the name, but I think it was something like 'Stormy Metropolis Money Launderers' (this massacre of the firm's name elicited a volley of giggles from Melody) – she saw a poor skunk being attacked by a ragdoll kitten and, feeling sorry for the defenseless polecat, opened the door just enough so the skunk could get inside.'" By this time, the two younger generations, having either personally experienced or heard the true story many times, were convulsed in laughter. Tweeners Ellen Annabelle and Elizabeth Emily, the two daughters of the second generation, could barely contain themselves; some minutes later they were still giggling as the adults attempted, without marked degrees of success, to appear more mature. Amidst the merriment, Annabelle Lacoste had breathed her last.

"We've met so many interesting people in our time, Ratio." In their more intimate moments, Melody had, early on in their marriage, begun calling her husband 'Ratio'. Horatio, on the other hand, thought the name, Melody, was already a cute name and that a nickname prettier than that would be hard to find. He occasionally called her "Mel" or "Dee". "Melodious" was rarer.

"Indeed, Mel, we have. As we sit here, watching the timeless waves roll into shore, I'm reminded of someone else who played an important role in our lives. I still think that one of the most selfless things you ever did was to choose Angelica, my babysitter, as your maid of honor at our wedding. You were such a popular girl in school and had many friends who would easily have qualified for that honor. But you chose Angelica. That act of kindness was a powerful demonstration of the love you had for me. But it also told me what a caring heart you had for those who aren't gifted in the commonly accepted ways. Remember how, whenever we invited Angelica to join us for an evening, she never failed, in her stilted raspy voice, to remind you of how much your selection of her for the honor meant to her. The story of your beautiful friendship with her went viral (as the young people say) throughout the community. No doubt that's why there were so many people at her funeral. Considering our age now, Angelica really did die very young. She was such a happy individual and she brought so much joy to people's lives – I believe, largely because of your demonstration of love for her."

"And," Horatio continued, "We can't forget Cherry. Despite her rough start in life and that infamous episode around the school bathroom fire, there's another example of your beautiful positive influence in the life of a young person. I could tell you many stories about my umpiring days with the high school boys baseball team. Travelling with them, I know they respected my calls and even respected me as a person, but I am positive that I didn't have nearly the effect on any one of them that you had on Cherry. I always remember feeling somewhat sorry for that plain-faced, morose little girl – but when you befriended her, not only did her whole outlook on life change, but her smile lit up the world around her and she even looked positively beautiful. People actually stopped calling her 'Cheerio'. She was no longer the sad, woebegone, girl everyone had known. She seemed to blossom when people started calling her 'Cherry'.

The fact that she asked you to be the matron of honor at her wedding to Jimmy – what was his last name? – oh, yes, Borthwick – really says it all in terms of her esteem for you. Jimmy wasn't from this area … I'm trying to remember how he and Cherry met. Hmm, oh yes, I remember. Jimmy had been part of the madrigal choir that came to Parkview School. I think their purpose was to promote the arts. I forgot to mention it to you, but I met Jimmy just before we left home to spend a couple of months here on this beautiful island. Of course, we knew that he and Cherry had started that little pastry and ice cream shop. Even though it had been broken into a couple of times, they persevered. Jimmy proudly told me that they were doing really well and had plans to expand within five or six years." Then, as an afterthought, Horatio added, "We should really go there more often. Remember how cute their little boys were – Mom and Dad standing proudly behind the counter as the little fellows, their hands encased in rubber gloves, so politely brought us our ice cream cones? I wish I could remember their names – I'm going to have to start writing things down."

A few more minutes went by as the individuals who, years ago, had become one, thought of the people they'd known. Then Melody, with an almost wistful recollection of days spent at her workplace, reminded herself and Horatio of the unforgettable people she'd gotten to work with and some of whom Horatio had gotten to know. "Remember Evadne Laverock? She was the woman who took an instant dislike to me when I arrived on the scene. Remember how I came to you and cried because of how she tried to turn the staff against me? As you well know, dear, I like to be at peace with everyone, but that was difficult with Evadne. Even though she had no direct influence on my work, she had all these little snide remarks directed at me or proclaimed loudly enough in my presence, ensuring I would hear her.

Then, one day, when Evadne had proclaimed something particularly hurtful to me, old Cedric Ravenshadow overheard her. He let her have it with both barrels. I could hardly believe that he had come to my defense in such a dramatic manner. I can still see the red anger mounting on his neck and reaching his face, then hearing him thunder, 'Ms. Laverock, I'm not unaware of how you've been bullying Melody without any provocation on her part. If I ever hear you saying anything negative towards her again, I'm sure I can talk Mr. Scrivens into firing you then and there.'

After that exchange, Evadne, although sullen for a few days, approached me the following Monday. For a moment, I feared what was coming. But I needn't have been concerned. I'll never forget her brokenhearted words, 'Melody, I am so very sorry. I know I've been treating you rotten right from the day you arrived on the scene. You were young, anxious to learn, and everyone liked you. I was sure you were after my job – although now that I think about it, why would anybody want to digitize old records all day long? Ravenshadow's warning the other day brought me to my senses. Things hadn't gone very well at home for years, and I guess something inside of me just flipped when I saw you. You were so young, so pretty, and had such a zest for life, and I envied you bitterly. I had absolutely no reason whatsoever to persecute you like I did. Will you please forgive me?' Of course, I did. I offered my arms for a hug and, although she hesitated for a split second, she almost knocked me down when she gave me a bear hug – I'm not sure a real bear could have hugged me more tightly."

"Is Evadne still around?" questioned Horatio. "Yep, she is, but she's in the Sunshine Nursing Home. She's 92 years old! Her mind is still sharp, but she is in a wheelchair. Not long before we left Chicago this last time, I'd been in touch with the nursing home and asked if I could speak with Evadne. I was told to call back another time because Evadne was instructing other residents how to use the computers that had been donated."

Again, they mused for a time, watching a kite-boarder skim over the waves, then catch a 5-foot wave just right, rise to 12 feet, somersault, and land gracefully, perfectly catching the next wave on the upslope. Then Horatio spoke, "I still think one of my favorite people memories is Rory. What a guy. And, what a great friend he turned out to be! Remember how shocked he was when we both approached him and I asked him to be the best man at our wedding? His family and ours had so many good times over the years. I don't think we've ever been to a White Sox game without them. Of course, although he denies it, we both know he always buys that 4-seat 25-game package specifically with us in mind. That humiliating experience with his repossessed Corvette really seemed to grab his attention. It's been so enjoyable watching him mature over the years. We all had a good chuckle when he, with legitimate and forgivable pride, observed, 'Now I'm the legitimate owner of a Corvette!' Only one of those cheerleaders didn't give up on him – Jasmine has been so good for him – and those boys of theirs, besides being attractive, were so well behaved. Let me think – I believe he'd been in that senior management position with the Chicago Board of Trade for more than 10 years before he finally retired. And, who would ever have thought that their Brady would've married our Ellen! For a while I thought Elizabeth might end up with Charlie, but that didn't work out – Thomas's arrival put an end to that budding relationship. But it all worked out for the best."

The weather was warming perceptibly, and the humidity was rising. Their coffee cups were empty, but their hearts were full.

"We've got so many good memories, Ratio, but I have an all-time favorite one." She paused, waiting for his reaction. Knowing that she had really asked the question in statement form, Horatio simply raised his left eyebrow in response. Melody continued, "My most cherished memory goes back to when our girls were probably only five and seven. Remember, how one beautiful late spring afternoon, you oh-so-secretly informed the girls (of course, you wanted me to hear what you told them), 'Do you kids like surprises?' Naturally, they responded with strong affirmatives! You told them that we were going to go for a drive. In typical childish fashion, they bombarded you with questions as we travelled towards the destination you had in mind. You just kept saying, 'You'll see.'

By the time you told them it would be just another mile or so, I had a pretty good idea of what you had in mind. Steelworkers Park. You led the three of us around, and then in back of the new tourism building and then down the beautiful flower-bordered walkway. And, sure enough, there were those tall oak trees. Two new benches had replaced the one we remembered from years gone by. Little Ellen was almost beside herself with glee, and Elizabeth was not far behind. The squirrels, sensing their excitement, raised their own chorus of chirps and barks. Between the girls and the squirrels, the chattering sounds were almost indistinguishable – you could almost imagine they were actually communicating with each other. The squirrels, with their flipping tails, even seemed to imitate the girls with their bouncing ponytails. When they finally exhausted themselves after chasing the squirrels and each other, they joined us on the opposite bench. Then our little thinker, Elizabeth, asked, 'Is this the surprise, Dad?' Your response was that it was just a part of the surprise. Almost simultaneously, they queried, 'What's the other part of the surprise?' When you told them the story of how you proposed to me, in this very place, that memorable night so long ago, their beautiful eyes grew bigger than ever as they sat in awe and wonder of the past of which they were not a part, but also of a future that would not forever remain a mystery."

In years yet to come, when Ellen and Elizabeth would themselves be grandparents, they would recall their parents' oft repeated, but spontaneous response, "It all worked out for the best."

THE END

ABOUT THE AUTHOR

Lorn Bergstresser has lived a life enriched by diverse experiences and meaningful contributions. Raised on a farm, and later returning to it, Lorn mastered a wide range of operations, from milking cows and operating machinery to self-taught welding and managing grain systems. In college he worked as a baker, a janitor, and a maintenance man. He earned a certificate in education and completed both BSc and MSc degrees, which led him to a career in research and development for an international chemical corporation.

With a passion for community service, Lorn devoted a decade to public school trusteeship at local, provincial, and national levels, and spent 24 years on the board of governors for a small university. An advocate for learning, he has taught certificate college courses in Myanmar and has traveled extensively.

Lorn's entrepreneurial spirit also flourished during his 16 years in sales and service with an international web conferencing business, servicing the blind and deaf communities. Since 2017, he has focused on editing books. Alongside his wife, Laura, Lorn divides his time between the gorgeous summers of southern Manitoba and the equally pleasant winters of South Padre Island, Texas.

Whether organizing sports in his hometown or exploring the world, Lorn cherishes every moment, embracing life with gratitude and joy.

A major thrust in the overall purpose of the Free Enterprise
Warriors Community is to tell the story of how the American
Free Enterprise System, in a little more than 250 years, has
transformed thousands of years of the world's Age of Wealth
Allocation into the Age of Wealth Creation.

This progress, with the opportunity and innovation it spurs,
makes real the previously outlandish idea of a janitor becoming a
millionaire. The tale told in this book is representative of countless
true to life experiences. It is our hope that, in the years to come,
millions of young people will experience lives based on solid
values and rational financial decisions.

Lorn's story illustrates that there are no magic tricks, no
artificial barriers, and no insurmountable challenges that can't be
overcome with grit, hard work, and by following a few simple rules.
It is not easy, but it is achievable, and that is the core lesson –
don't let anyone tell you the North American Dream is
not possible for you!

FreeEnterpriseWarriors.com

THESE NUMBERS DON'T LIE

Thanks to our nation's amazing Free Enterprise System, the stunning success achieved by Horatio and his wife in pursuing their dream would be unbelievable – if it wasn't for the fact that it continues to happen over and over again!

While our hero is fictional, he is truly representative of millions who have moved from poverty to economic security through their own diligent efforts.

Millionaire Janitor does not present a popular message for those who would have us believe that the American Dream is dead. Nor is this tale for those who confidently assert that there is no point in making the effort to achieve this very realistic aim. Our work has one central, focused, goal – to encourage each individual to understand the rewards awaiting them when they conscientiously pursue their dream.

Based on this clear purpose, on our website we have provided a working spreadsheet which you can download to review the assumptions and calculations used to show Horatio's and Melody's financial progress. You can test these assumptions and even do your own "what-ifs" by going to the link below or scanning the QR code, then downloading the spreadsheet and explanatory document.

Enjoy!

Download the Spreadsheet that explains
Horatio's journey here.

LornBergstresser.com

THE AMERICAN DREAM TRILOGY

I must admit that while extensive reading of books of all kinds has always given me great pleasure, there never was a lifelong plan to become an author. Perhaps finding myself agreeing to edit many books late in life was a subconscious movement in that direction. However, once I was privileged to become an advisor to the team at Free Enterprise Warriors, my imagination took wings.

Gaining a fresh appreciation for the importance of the Free Enterprise concept, discussions with several FEW members inspired me to show just how realistic and achievable are the amazing results of the fabled American Dream. Misquoting a popular phrase, I felt it was important to emphasize, "The rumors of the death of the American Dream are greatly exaggerated!"

The pleasure derived from this first effort, and its gratifying responses, has led to additional research into the topic. Working with my many friends and the team at FEW, I am pleased to announce the pending publication of the second book in the series, "Diamond Nine". This work further explores the rewards and challenges of seeking to capitalize on the opportunities within the most powerful economic system the world has ever known.

The abundant material we have collected will be summarized in the final book of the American Dream series, "Ruby's Jewels: From the Ashes of Adversity to Sharing the Bounty." This book will explore how the present generations are responsible for the greatest distribution of wealth that the world has ever seen.

CHAPTER 1　THE BIG BLAST

In the sultry Sage Park Stadium, the crack of the bat meeting the 90 mile-per-hour fastball head-on reverberated like a split-second thunderclap following a lightning strike. No one in the announced crowd of 2265 even considered the possibility that a ball struck with that ferocity would remain within the confines of the field. Despite the humidity, the ball carried well beyond the fence, bouncing off a semi-trailer while it was rapidly approaching the ramp to join the expressway. It was a two-run walk-off homer.

As the fire-balling closing pitcher, aptly named Ryder Cannon, despondently dropped to his haunches, knowing he had left that fastball way too high in the zone, the hometown fans erupted in rapturous cheers, high-fiving and hugging both friends and strangers. Canyon Ridge manager Carlos "Capi" Mendoza, in consultation with his pitching coach, Donnie "Buck" Donovan, had agreed to shorten Ryder's days off to give their beloved Rattlers a chance in the fifth and deciding playoff game against the high-flying Sandstone Bay Stallions. The move had been logical. But unsuccessful.

Ryder, now 18, had developed quickly, both in pitching ability and in physical prowess. He had created quite a stir while still in the under-16 league in western Texas. At the tender age of 14 he had already been hurling fastballs at 72 mph. Now, barely 4 years older, he was developing into what major-league scouts commonly referred to as "a talent". And, Ryder was, indeed, referred to a great deal. "Height 6'5", still growing. Weight 198. Throws left. Fastball is 'go-to' pitch, but owns an effective sweeping curve, and a more-than-adequate change-up. Lots of potential." These words, and many like them, were reported to Triple A teams, and some of those mouth-watering rumors even made it to "the bigs". Three major league teams had Ryder on their "watch this guy" list.

Ryder had been given a 1-run lead in the top of the ninth. Score: 3-2. This home run in the bottom of the ninth by Logan Hardwick, the Stallions' third baseman, locally eulogized as "The Wall", had not been in the Rattlers' game plan. All the contests in the 5-game series had been nail-biters. The series had been tied by the Stallions back in Canyon Ridge. In that fourth game, they'd earned the winning run in the 6th inning on a suicide squeeze. No one had scored a run after that.

Now, this had happened.

The game was over. For the Rattlers, the season was over.

Not so for the Stallions. They had lived to play another series, this time their opponent would be either the Thunder Mesa Mustangs or the Copperfield Wranglers. At the moment, though, no one was thinking beyond the instant that was already history.

Meanwhile, the sorrow … and the exhilaration … continued. With heads downcast and some tears evident the Rattler players and staff disconsolately watched the exuberant "mob dance" of the winning team, then turned to watch the fans who were exulting in an unremitting celebration of joy, hugging friends and strangers alike. Finally, trailing sporadically behind their managers, then 'bucking up', the losing team proceeded to shake hands with the winners. Winning pitcher, Cole Firestone, strode up to the still downcast Ryder, man-hugged him and said simply, "I've been there. It hurts, I know." They shook hands, Ryder impulsively gave Cole another hug, this time in bearlike fashion, and they separated, each going their own way.

Little did these young men, strangers, realize that life was more than baseball. They had much to learn. And … not only about baseball. Not only these two, but 26 others who loved to participate in "America's Pastime" were to realize that life was about more than baseball. Much more.